NORTH SHORE HORIZONS
PO Box 206
Two Harbors, MN 55616

EVERY EIGHTEEN SECONDS

A Journey Through Domestic Violence

By Nancy Kilgore

VOLCANO PRESS

Library of Congress Cataloging-in-Publication Data
Nancy Kilgore, 1949–
    Every eighteen seconds: a journey through domestic violence / by Nancy Kilgore.—1st Volcano Press ed.
        p.   cm.
    Previously published: Eugene, OR: Learning Information for Today, 1983.
    Includes bibliographical references.
    ISBN 0-912078-99-5 : $8.95
    1. Kilgore, Nancy, 1949– . 2. Abused wives—United States—Biography.
I. Title. II. Title: Every eighteen seconds.
HV6626.2.K55 1993
362.82'92'092—dc20
[B]   93-19181
                                                                      CIP

Volcano Press participates in the Cataloging in Publication program of the Library of Congress. However, in our opinion, the data provided above by CIP for this book does not adequately nor accurately reflect the book's scope and content. Therefore, we are offering our librarian and bookstore users the choice between CIP's treatment and an Alternative CIP prepared by Sanford Berman, Head Cataloger at Hennepin County Library, Edina, Minnesota.

Alternative Cataloging-in-Publication Data
Kilgore, Nancy, 1949–
Every eighteen seconds: a journey through domestic violence. 1st Volcano Press ed. Volcano, CA: Volcano Press, 1993, copyright 1992.
First published by Learning Information for Today.
Consists of letters by a battered woman to her son, each followed by "self-help education" data. Includes foreword by Del Martin.
1. Kilgore, Nancy, 1949– . 2. Battered women—Personal narratives. 3. Battered women—Self-help materials. 4. Mother and son—Personal narratives. 5. Mother's letters. 6. Woman battering—Prevention. I. Title. II. Title: Every eighteen seconds. III. Title: A journey through domestic violence. IV. Volcano Press. V. Martin, Del. Foreword.
362.882

Design, production, and typesetting: Brenda Anderson, Marketing Concepts.
Editorial: Ann Sharkey.

Please enclose $8.95 for each copy of *Every Eighteen Seconds* ordered. For postage and handling, please include $4.50 for the first book and $1.00 for each additional book. California residents add appropriate sales tax. Please contact Volcano Press for quantity discount prices, and write for our complete domestic violence catalogs.

Volcano Press, Inc., P.O. Box 270-E, Volcano, CA 95689-0270.
Telephone: (209) 296-3445 Fax (209) 296-4515

Foreword

Back in 1975 when I first announced that I was writing a book called *Battered Wives,* people quickly changed the subject. Erin Pizzey had exposed wife-beating as a significant social problem in Britain, but no one was about to admit that it also happened here in the United States to the same alarming degree..."every eighteen seconds."

Since then many books have been written about battered women that provide statistics, research data, profiles of batterers and their victims, information on the law and its enforcement, tips on counseling and community resources, etc. These books are technical and directed primarily to the professions, service providers and related community agencies. They do not have popular appeal.

Nancy Kilgore has personalized "the problem" for us in a series of letters to her son. These letters are an intimate account of what happened between his mother and father, available for him to read and draw his own conclusions when he is old enough to understand. It was written while the memory was fresh, before the rationalizations of time faded the colors of anger and violence.

Kilgore tells her story simply and honestly. She shares her experience of abuse, her feelings of despair, her ambivalence, the difficulties she encountered in her resolve to make a new life. This isn't the sob story of a martyred victim. Kilgore gets in touch with her own anger and reaches certain insights about herself.

I, for one, thank Nancy Kilgore for her courage and her willingness to share her story with all of us. It is in the sharing that others may experience vicariously the reality of domestic violence and be moved to help us break the cycle of violence that is passed on from one generation to the next.

Hopefully, Nancy Kilgore's son will be spared. Hopefully, too, our sons and grandsons will be instilled with a sense of self-worth and self-assertiveness that transcends the need for violence as self expression.

Del Martin
San Francisco, California

Contents

Dedication & Acknowledgments

This book is dedicated to my son. You have given me direction and insight. Without you I would never have been called "Mama."

I also want to acknowledge Oliver Johnson. You helped me see how children's hearts and eyes are so open to the events of their lives. Your determination guides me to help adults see the scenes with the eyes of a child. God has a special job for you.

My thoughts are with those victims of domestic violence who have Post Traumatic Stress Syndrome. I hope you find the path that leads to serenity and purpose. May the emotional numbness and state of being jumpy and irritable be replaced with safety and trust.

I am deeply indebted to all friends who gave me the gift of inspiration to go onward.

This book is dedicated to all the isolated women who live in houses that have slamming doors and heart-sonnet cries.

May this book be a memorial to all the women and children who have died and who will die in the cycle of domestic violence.

Dear Reader:

I want a special privilege from you. I ask that your attention and concern be focused on an ungovernable problem from which millions of prisoners still suffer right now. These everyday prisoners do not bear any distinguishing marks on their sleeves. The suffering and deaths of this great army of unknown victims have never been accurately recorded.

This is the inside story of a personal experience of hell reconstructed by a survivor. I am a formerly battered woman who prayed that I would not be murdered in my own home. Many women share my experience and have fears of being beaten to death. They are being brutally beaten without mercy by their husbands or male partners.

I hope I will contribute toward raising your understanding of domestic violence.

I want you to know who I am and who I am not. I can assure you I am not a professional writer or social worker who has a degree from a university. My credentials come from a terrifying life experience which forced me to evaluate myself. I believe I am a person with a wisdom acquired through my background. Since my battering, I have taught social workers, counselors, and ministers how to understand and effectively work with abused women. I feel very strongly that I have much in common with many who are now reading these words.

Though my abuse was severe, many men and women will catch glimpses of themselves.

My intent in revealing the following intimate journal written to my son, is to share a devastating experience. The words will be only shadows of my memories. To expose a way of life that no one deserves to live, I have paid with my blood. I miss being able to use my real name. I am in seclusion because the law does not protect me. Freedom is no longer a reality for me. My appreciation of its preciousness emanates from a first-hand understanding of its rarity. Even though I am painfully aware of the ineffectiveness of laws that do not give battered women the confidence to believe in them, I do not advocate building more prisons or stirring up hysteria and hatred toward men. By sharing a very personal journal with you, I hope our society will see that a frightening reality needs to be exposed.

I do not believe that we are living in a doomed time. If only a small percentage of this world will see the blackness and the scope of battering, the insight will be phenomenal. Awareness of this problem is a key to the evolutionary progress our society must make if it is to understand the war which rages within our species and to explore the possibilities of peaceful sexual coexistence. I appeal to all people to understand the urgent need to bridge the division of the sexes. Most of those now involved in listening and talking about battering are women. Women alone cannot stop this crime. Men must learn about it before it's too late and before the next victim is their mother, sister, wife, or daughter. In the name of many women who daily suffer in silence, I beg for concern.

I wrote the following journal to my son nearly twelve years ago to share with him what really happened. It is a gift to him and a message for other victims as well as all men and women who want to understand the phenomenon. I now live in Oregon and facilitate support groups and workshops. For those who seek illumination on this topic, the way is open.

After each letter you will find **Self-Help Education (SHE).** These sections will increase your self-awareness and understanding of domestic violence. This information is in numerical order and can be found in the back of this book.

Nancy Kilgore

Dear Son:

On that night of your birth, I began to plead with the nurse again. "Please, I can't stand the pain!" She didn't seem to listen. I closed my eyes and believed that I was at a still point in eternity. I felt alone. Very softly with the tips of my fingers I circled my stomach. My eyes were open. My whole body quivered from exhaustion. I struggled with a force of nature. The pressure between my legs was unbearable. I wondered how such pain could be the result of legs that I once opened during satisfying pleasure. I yelled long animal howls of anguish as I pushed and pushed. As I closed my eyes, the last current pulsed through my womb with such a strong thrust that I saw colors of bright orange and purple. In the mirror I suddenly saw the deliverance of my baby all glistening with water and blood. The feeling was beyond description.

My eyes danced when I first saw the free verse of your body. Is this gorgeous baby really mine? By giving birth to you, dormant qualities uncurled that were latent in me. It was through your birth that I can say I finally met myself. I am head over heels in love with you. You are a spectrum of divine perfection. I want no one else to raise you. You are a gem; a mirror that is rare.

My son, today you kissed me for the first time. In receiving this simple expression, the feeling I have for you has increased tenfold. For so long I thought I was the only one in this relationship who gave, gave, gave, gave. You have inspired me to write. I am travelling again and am absolutely electrified and restless. Before this day, I had such an urge to write. I wrote on the back of record albums, on envelopes, in books, in newspapers, on match books, on kleenex, on toilet paper: on buses, in cars, at cafe tables, talking to a friend on the phone...anywhere to connect me on my journey back to life. Writing to you, today, seems like I have reopened a trunkful of memories from an unhappy past. Writing to you helps me cope with what happened.

Something is niggling at me, something terrible just below the surface of my conscious mind. I don't want to recall that awful night, but I am tormented by split-second images that stab into my present. My mind is filled with a crazy kaleidoscope of events. There are so many blank spots. Flashes of clarity disappear before I can make sense of them. Something is so ugly that I can't bear to face it. I call suicide lines constantly. It is a time when the only people I can talk to are separated from me by telephone wire. I am lost, pacing from wall to wall, in one never-ending corridor of torment.

Little one, you know nothing of the hard fight for existence we as fugitives have had. I have been controlled by one piercing obsession: to keep you and me alive. Some people lodge themselves permanently in the same postage stamp-sized piece of earth and are content to remain an entire lifetime. You and I, however, have known constant change since we both journeyed one unforgettable night from hell. I imposed a sense of order in our lives. But one night of holocaust, July 21, 1979, destroyed our rational universe and our lives were thrown into a vast chaotic disorder. I know I have had a nervous breakdown catalyzed by that night.

I guess it's hard for parents to admit why they love their children. It's hard for me to admit loving the whole task of raising you.

With your new naked eyes, you can see so many radiant and pulsating feasts. You stare so long and intently at the trees and giggle when you look up at their large and heavy branches. The large leaves that glide down are your toys. You live in a land of flowers and play.

Inside of me there is still a young girl who is wailing above a pool of pain. This pain has cut deep into my heart with steel barbed wire.

At this time in my life, I feel ill-equipped to handle you or the fear. I admit that I do not know how to live with fear. This fear is something that I've tried to make go away. Through this fear, I have become aware of my body: My intestines tighten, the sound of my voice changes, and my body movements are affected. I cry for no apparent reason. Little in my childhood conditioning has helped prepare me for this fear. My mental efforts to stop this fear are as helpful as a broken umbrella in a windy downpour. My fear of being recognized is all pervading. I have fear that I shall be killed if I go and cast my ballot, eat in a restaurant, or walk down the street. My fear of the past forbids me to live in the present. I do no know whether to move right or left, up or down, or stand still. When and where will the giant redwood fall? I am continually enmeshed by fear. There is a great fear in living: the seeds of my fear are from the past.

Love, Mom

Self-Help Education: Read SHE 1 on page 79.

Dear Son:

I felt like a political exile as my eyes studied the white cabinets filled with medical instruments and bottles. There was a strong disinfectant smell. I wondered if this was the precinct of hell. I wondered what would become of me as I lay on the vinyl examining table.

I wanted to run away and escape but Terri, the counselor who had been assigned to me through the shelter, kept assuring me with a patient kindness, "There, there, it's over. You're safe. He's not here." I sobbed as she comforted me. The room echoed.

As a young doctor surveyed the bruises on my body he said, "You know, you can file charges against this Greg guy. You have a pretty bad whiplash, and these purple, bulging bruises didn't get there from playing hopscotch."

I noticed a sharp pain in the small of my back as I said, "I know you mean well, but I can't report him. He is the father of my son. Everything got out of control."

"Look, you do what you want. Take this pill. It will calm you down. I'll put twelve of them in a bottle. You can take them at the shelter. You're going to need them, little lady. You just had the shit knocked out of you." I swallowed the pill as my hands shook holding a paper cup of water. The water dribbled down my chin and down the front of my yellow hospital gown. The left side of my face was numb and had no feeling. My tongue studied the inside of my mouth and stopped when I found a chipped tooth. I felt so exposed, as if my personal dignity had been annihilated. Dying seemed so enticing. I felt more dead than alive.

I could not repress my instant hatred of the shelter and thought it wasn't appropriate for me. I was still denying that I was a battered woman.

In a bathroom mirror I viewed my body with no clothes. I wanted no part of that torn dress. I felt an uncontrollable spasm as my body tried to puke; it was painful when I couldn't throw up. I felt like such a failure. I realized why they locked up my twelve pills. A nameless terror kept returning and slicing through my body: suicidal thoughts tumbled around in my brain. I knew that I had to make a decision to live right then and there.

Those first few hours seemed thin and one-dimensional. The hours seemed like jagged pieces of broken glass. All that had formerly been my life was far away. As I looked out the window and directed my thoughts to the southeast, in the direction of our home, I could see only the moon. I felt my entire body pierced with a dull pain that found no relief in a sigh or a tear. So many horrible images flashed through my brain. The sound track from our fight had not been erased. I kept repeating to myself as I squeezed the curtain, "I am, I am, I am..."

As my head throbbed from a lack of sleep, I felt like I was sentenced to a prison of incredible weariness. Even when I finally crashed and fell asleep after three days of sleeplessness, I woke up incredibly tired. It was hard to make sense out of anything, realizing that just a couple of days ago I lived with your father. I kept saying to myself, "Where am I?" I couldn't taste food. The sight of solid food made me ill. I was so incredibly thirsty; I drank glass after glass of orange juice. I switched to Pepsi because the caffeine kept me going.

On the second day of my stay in the shelter, the woman director came into my room and told me that my sister was on the phone. "She sounds pretty insistent. I think your family is probably pretty curious to know what has happened to you. Just pick up the receiver. It's in the wash room."

I agreed to meet my family at a shopping center near the shelter. I felt so apprehensive about meeting them. I felt like I would die of humiliation. I didn't know how to begin to tell them what had happened. One of the counselors agreed to come with me. Her name was Marlene. She looked young and radical. Her intuitive question amazed me, "Isn't it hard to talk to family, especially after something like this has happened?" I felt a strength come from her.

When my mother first saw me she backed away and put her hand to her cheek as if she'd been struck. For a moment her expression seemed to be frozen with fright. I was wearing a wrinkled skirt and a dirty lime-colored blouse that someone had donated to the shelter. My whole family tried so hard to hide their nervousness and apprehension. I felt an enormous sense of relief when my older sister held me in her arms and comforted me by saying, "I love you!" Tears squeezed out of my eyes. My pain became more intense when I saw how strong my mother wanted to be for me.

"Don't you think we could talk about this someplace else?" my mother said. Marlene told us that we could drive to a nearby river and talk.

Everyone was so silent as we drove. I sat in between my mother and the counselor. My mother was unable to speak as she held my hand. She turned her head toward the window and fought back tears. It felt so strange to be close to my family. I felt so humiliated. A small knot was in my stomach. Over my left eye I felt the most excruciating headache.

When we were young and giggly in bed, my older sister would hold the book high so I could see the pictures. It was hard to believe that my older sister, now, was trembling. I felt such a desire to hold her. My desire ceased when she turned her head around with a puzzled face and looked at me in the back seat. Her words hit me with an over-powering directness. "You had better come home. You have to think about your son. What can you do? Go on welfare? Your life is in shambles!" My desire to trust her stopped. Suddenly, Marlene in-terrupted my sister, "I don't think it's a good idea for her to come and live with any one of you. If I were you, I would be on the lookout for Greg. He will probably be looking for Nancy at your homes. I didn't want to tell Nancy yet, but Greg knocked down three doors last night looking for her. She is lucky to be in the shelter and alive today." Every-one seemed to gasp and a long silence followed. "When he found out Nancy had left the house last night, he was arrested for disturbing the peace in the neighborhood."

I asked myself, "Why wasn't he arrested for what he had done to me? Why hadn't anyone called the police? Why didn't the police come when my peace was destroyed?" Everything seemed so unjust and ironic.

"Most men who do this to a woman, even when they are fully prosecuted, usually get off with a mis-demeanor. Misdemeanor means only a one month jail sentence," said the counselor.

My sister, in a very quizzical and self-righteous tone of voice said, "I go to church every Sunday and this doesn't happen to anyone I know. All the women I know have nice husbands." I sensed an angry undercurrent in her voice as her eyes glared at me.

Marlene spoke with such candor, "It's speculated that over fifty percent of all relationships have some physical violence. It isn't only poverty-stricken women who get beaten because battering has no class lines. Forty percent of all calls for police assistance are for husband-wife disputes. Representing only the reported, at least 1.8 million women are known to suffer from wife-beating. A woman is beaten every eighteen seconds in her own home."

Love, Mom

Self-Help Education: Re-read SHE 1 on page 79; try to memorize at least two statistics.

Dear Son:

At the shelter, everyone seemed to congregate in the kitchen. There was always some activity going on: a mother frying hamburger, a child being spanked, a mother washing dishes. The counter tops were green. It was there that I first communicated with another battered woman.

Mary's eyes were black and blue. One eye was nearly swollen shut. Her nose was in a splint. I noticed her surveying my wounds and her eyes suddenly filled with tears. A knowing look was exchanged and we spontaneously hugged each other. We both felt such a bond of compassion. No words were spoken. They were not needed.

For the eleven days I was in the shelter, I walked around with my stomach in knots. I craved to be alone with my thoughts. To think coherently was very difficult. I felt like a sieve because I couldn't seem to hold onto any of my thoughts. The windows of my life were open and I felt the pain of a million stares.

I can recall looking at a woman who was holding a bottle of shampoo. She had a dab of mayonnaise on her protruding lower lip. Her belly was round and pregnant. "Do you want to wash your hair?" she said. "You can borrow my shampoo."

"My hair," I replied weakly. I had forgotten to comb my hair for such a long time that I wondered, how long. Her voice brought me back to the present.

"Look," she said sincerely, "I see your bruises. You're no different than me. My husband slammed my back against a washing machine. The doctor says I have a blood clot on my kidney. I look pretty good today. Sometimes I looked like a piece of raw ground beef. I hope the baby is going to be OK."

Another woman walked into the room. Her front teeth were knocked out. She said, matter-of-factly, "You know, your baby looks kind of hungry. We share our food here. We know you probably don't have any money. Most of us didn't get out with money. You have just joined the biggest sorority in the world. A lot of us don't make our membership public, though."

The look of her club was appalling to me...a club where women licked their wounds.

I learned to no longer be naive, frightened, or offended by other people. I started to see that relationships could be coarse and gritty for other women as well. I realized that class and social status ceased at the shelter's front door. I met a woman who played the cello and a woman who belonged to the Hell's Angels. My education about battering contin-

ued when I was given books to read. The book
that educated me the most was *Battered Wives*[1].

I felt a sort of curiosity come over me about how
we handled the grimness of it all. It wasn't uncom-
mon to hear one of us laugh for no reason. A friend
of mine told me that Greg had completely torn up
the house. She described what she had seen there,
"I hesitated to go in at first. I tried the door and it
just swung open. Greg broke all the legs on the
table. The stereo is smashed into little tiny tooth-
picks. He kicked in the TV screen. He put ketchup
and mustard all over the walls. He threw out all the
contents of the kitchen cabinets and drawers. All
the windows in the living room are broken. There
are several walls with holes in them. The place looks
like an animal went through it." She paused and
then said with a sudden urgency in her voice, "I
suggest you come and get your things right now.
He's not there." I can remember laughing uncontrollably as I spoke, "I can't handle picking any of
my things up right now. I don't care about anything."

I think most of us in the shelter suffered from
an inferiority complex. We weren't treated with any
value in our homes and in this setting we felt even
more like nonentities. For many of us there was no
material link with our former lives. All we had was
our naked existence...ourselves. We had dealt with
the constant threat of death looming over our heads
in our own homes. Many of us felt that we had no

1. Martin, Del, *Battered Wives*, Volcano Press, Inc., Volcano, CA, 1981.

future. I kept telling myself that I had a history, a life before this place. I am sure that the idea of suicide was entertained by almost everyone.

I wanted to die. Sometimes I slept to escape my mental torment. I always woke up to the shrill sounds of my roommates' children. Some of my most private hours were spent in the middle of the night when all the other women were sleeping. I felt I had some privacy when I stayed awake all night. An inner voice inside me was not consoling as it whispered that my life was the mirror of a loser.

After many sleepless nights, I was extremely irritable and yearned for privacy. I wanted to bathe in my own home without having to feel that someone had bathed before me and hadn't cleaned the tub. I wanted to lie naked in my own bed and lock the door so no one could come in unannounced.

Sometimes when I went inside to find respite from all the disgust and the ugliness that surrounded me, I found a boundless longing for a nostalgic time when your father and I held each other tightly, lovingly. When my mind was given free rein, it clung to his image. There were times when I couldn't determine if his image was real or not. I saw him smile as he said, "I love you. I need you." I cried a lot. I cried for my losses...Greg and the loss of me.

Survival doesn't care how you survive. I found it had no integrity, no conscience, nor compassion.

I had to pay for my room at the shelter. The only money I had was forty dollars that my mother had given me. I knew she couldn't give me anymore. I hoarded that money; it had to stretch for us. At first it was tremendously hard to "accept charity." My head was lowered as a nun gave me milk for your formula, eight plums, two large red tomatoes, rice, and dried beans. I kept telling myself, "Survival has no pride...survival has no pride." Anything that was not connected with the immediate task of keeping us alive had lost its value. I was stripped of all my middle-class Protestant ethics and went on welfare.

Welfare made me more depressed. The social worker had snappy little eyes and a pudgy face. He reminded me of an experienced FBI agent with all of his questions. I had to sign papers that said I no longer would live with your father. I signed papers that stated that your father was mentally incompetent and that the district attorney could not approach him for child support. I truly believed that your father had gone over the fine line of sanity. When all the papers had been signed, I laid my head down on top of them and cried. I felt like I had signed your father out of our lives. Our survival depended on those papers. There was no choice.

I did talk to your father on the phone while I was at the shelter. It was the last time I ever heard his voice. The conversation was hard to follow. I felt dumb-witted. As he spoke to me in a voice that almost pierced my eardrum, I kept pinching myself.

"You took, you took me, you bitch." I felt so sorry for him. He had lost his mind. It took a great deal of effort to keep listening to him and not speak back in an anger that had festered underneath my skin like a boil. I knew he would no longer yell at me when I said, "Greg, there is no hope for us. I am tired of being hit like a dog!"

He could not talk. I heard him sobbing and I visualized him sitting on the floor. My heart went out to him. I cried aloud, "I'm not trying to punish you. I am afraid of you and your anger." I hung up the phone and felt very empty as I went back to my room. I had never wanted to ruin him. In his mind he thought that I had destroyed his whole world. From my viewpoint, he had done the same to my world. I had to exclude him from our lives forever.

My legs seemed to buckle when I walked out of the shelter with a letter that said: "In our opinion, because Greg Layton has been abusive on several occasions, it would be dangerous for him to know Nancy's whereabouts." Those words brought me to a chilling reality. In order to survive we would have to go into hiding. It became vividly clear to me that I could never again speak to him.

It was hard to grasp at first; my consciousness had a difficult time accepting the fact that freedom was mine when I left the shelter. It was hard to feel that I still belonged to the world. I was totally un-prepared for many of the tasks that lay ahead of me. I did feel a relief to leave a past where I feared that I would be killed in my own home. The intensity of that fear was similar to the pain of a dentist's drill without the benefit of novocaine.

Love, Mom

Self-Help Education: Read SHE 2 on page 81. Write a paragraph about how you have been abused.

Letter Four

Dear Son:

I find my appearance quite unique this morning. I am starting to look a little primitive. Mascara and freshly washed hair are becoming alien to me. Spaghetti sauce is speckled on a nightgown that I have worn for two days.

I am not aware of the passage of time and I am not thinking about joining anyone for lunch today. I have burrowed myself in this apartment, doing whatever suits me. I like feeling irresponsible and I feel I have a legitimate excuse to sit in bed, eat spaghetti, or pace the perimeter of this room. I am in no mood to take a woodland walk. I am in the eye of a tornado and all I can do is hold on. My tired psyche wants to tune its system up again and understand the puzzle of my life. This room is my sanitarium.

It appears to me that I am beginning to lose my mind. The other day in a store I could not understand how to make change. It isn't hard to detect the symptoms in my appearance. There is no one who can harbor me or understand that my heart has been broken past all mending. No one's verbal sympathy can help I do not want to hear anyone's words vibrate on my ear's tympanic membrane. The phone has been unplugged for two weeks. An internal civil war has invaded every cell in my brain.

I am not just another frantic young mother. There is an uproar of emotions that make these words flow from me. I have a stigma. For so long I have suffered in silence. Like all battered women, I have had my intelligence and sanity questioned repeatedly. I am aching to be understood. I feel comfortable writing because talking has failed. Writing seems to keep my life from decaying into a subhuman existence. Lately, my happiness with human beings has been so unfulfilling. Many meaningful people have left me behind. I have been let down. My bones feel frozen inside.

I have gotten a distinct feeling from those that I associate with that I am threatening and a little crazy. As I write, Judy Collins is a good companion; she sings to me in the background. It is such a lonely time. I do feel peaceful at this writing. I am so glad to be out of the war zone. There is a woman across the street who is playing the piano and the notes are drifting over and sending good feelings. I feel a simple happiness to live today in my simple surroundings. My living room is my bedroom and my kitchen has brown linoleum peeling away from its floor. I feel a sense of security being here as my unknown secrets emerge.

We live in a ground-floor apartment in an old frame house. I am getting to know myself better. It's Thanksgiving and the leaves are cluttering up the street gutters. I don't feel like gathering round the symbolic stuffed bird. I do not want to be at the family table ringed with crystal bowls of candied

yams and cranberries. Yesterday, for quick nourish-
ment I punctured a can of butterscotch milk shake.
Today, even stale Cheez-its or an oversoaked salad
from yesterday would appear as a treasure to my
starving stomach.

A friend brought over a half-gallon of milk the
other morning. I knew we were poor when I delighted like a little girl at pouring it into a shiny wine
glass and savoring it. We hardly see fresh fruit. You
and I can make one orange last two days. It is such
a celebration! We laugh so much. I pretend that
your orange section is a miniature spaceship that
deceptively flies away just as you reach to grasp it.

There are days for me that never end. I cannot
sleep worrying about the bills and feeling guilty that
you were thrust into this barren world. There is something that helps me escape…a Humpty Dumpty lamp.
I love this lamp. I need it here on top of my writing
desk. It does not have a lowly place amongst the
typewriter, baby bottle, and paper. It is in the highest strata; it crowns my writing territory and brings
joy to me. It evokes memories of my childhood.

I have to admit that Humpty Dumpty was not
my favorite tale. Mine were *Cinderella* and *Sleeping
Beauty*. These stories still seem to flow through the
pathways of my brain, evoking the same ironic
questions: Where is my love? Where is my prince?
When will I know the true enchantment of "we"
and "thou"?

Time has been so unrelenting on these thirty journeys around the sun. Yesterday, I methodically drizzled a fine thread of honey into my tea. I felt my life was oozing away. I deserve this time to understand who I really am. The dishes can wait. I want equilibrium back in my life. Little tugging fingers on my skirt hem can wait too. How can I love you when I think no one loves me? How can I answer your needs when no one wants to hear mine? I am looking for clarification.

The world into which I was born was rapidly expanding. Pearls were in. It was a time when cigarette manufacturers manipulated the American public to smoke by inserting coupons redeemable for valuable gifts. Life Savers were five cents and came in very limited flavors. Playtex girdles came into being when a new fiber enabled the girdle to stretch. Kotex ads were just starting to appear in magazines. Popular car names were the Studebaker and De Soto. The human mind was just starting to be released from mathematical drudgery by IBM. Unions were well established. Gimmicks bombarded the American housewife. Hand soap was advertised with a free wash cloth and laundry detergent was pushed with the enticement of a free glass. Toni had twin contests. It was a time when the American public started trying to understand the confusing atomic warfare.

Love, Mom

Self-Help Education: Read SHE 3 on page 83. If you feel that you might need these numbers in the future, write them on a piece of paper and put them in your wallet. Read SHE 4 on page 84. Write a paragraph about what characteristics you can relate to in yourself.

Dear Son:

I do not consider myself a masochist and was not physically abused as a child.

I wish I could "compartmentalize" what I'm like. I've never been religious in any orthodox sense. My own personal religion seems to be more spiritual than philosophic. I have never liked criticism or restrictions; I like to live by impulse and improvisation. My favorite color is purple and I adore spicy scents like iris and cinnamon. I love lipstick. My class ring is still on my finger. I still believe in love. There is a part of me that likes to be taken care of. I am a child in so many ways. Tony the Tiger's frosted flakes are still G-R-R-E-A-T with me.

When I awoke this morning, warm sunshine came through the window. I loved sitting in its warmth without a thread on my body. When I stood up and gazed at a full length mirror, I noticed that I had lost weight. I found myself accepting what I saw, even that annoying little hair on my chin. My hips and thighs were still concentrated with some extra weight. My breasts were round and had started to sag a little at their sides. I found myself realizing that I no longer lived in the childhood space of innocence when I noticed my facial reflection was as rigid as a jack-o-lantern.

As I write, I am aware that my thinking is triggered by past associations. It seems that I'm in that quiet child's room where the yellow sun races across the wooden floor and illuminates the sparkling, restless dust. As a child, I accepted myself as a future mommy to the exclusion of any other possibility. My first doll reinforced that I would never blossom into full womanhood until I was a mother.

Going back in time seems easier than living in the present. I am struggling for peace of mind. On my journey back, I feel like a detective who does not want to miss any clue that might be a rock or tide in the ocean of my life. I can almost see the chalk marks on the sidewalk. My relationship to my mother was enormously important. She was the model I would expect myself to become.

Memories seem to be colliding over each other and want to be recalled. My mind keeps parceling out a 1950s film of a past security and happiness with her.

Everything seemed to be associated with smell then. I recall the smell of laundry that was dried by the sun's rays and the aroma coming from my mother's kitchen with chicken stewing and cookies baking. One of my earliest memories is memorizing her with my eyes as she patiently pressed a fork vertically and horizontally on peanut butter cookies. Sitting next to her warm body and smelling her hands that had been seasoned with garlic from past meat loaf dinners was the highest honor.

I grew up in suburbia with purple pansies growing in our front yard. My childhood was spent playing house with a miniature ironing board, refrigerator, dust mop, sink, and stove. As I played, my
mother anxiously awaited my father's return from
work each day. I grew up seeing how her day re-
volved around my father's homecoming. She sup-
pressed her own desires and wished to eagerly
please him. I never saw my mother angry at my
father. They never fought.

I was a very passive and phobic little girl, a spec-
tator. The outside world seemed so threatening and
forbidding. I was afraid to roller-skate or climb trees.
During my childhood, whenever the slightest twinge
of anger filled and gnawed within me, the message
had been implanted: nice girls do not show anger.

At night I would ask the moon that nothing
would ever happen to my mother. Her love was
something I was afraid to lose. I wanted desper-
ately to hold onto it. I confided in my mother.

I felt dreadfully sorry for her. She arranged her
life in accordance with what was best for her family. Sunday was a day when she seemed happiest:
It was a day that breathed of togetherness and family. During the weekdays, she looked abandoned
and unfulfilled as her life was mercilessly sucked
away by the roar of the vacuum cleaner, repairmen
who made her wait, and a television show called
"Queen for a Day." Many times she was trapped in
the house listening to coughs, mopping up spilled

milk, making raspberry jello with miniature marshmallows, hugging and cuddling four little girls, and refereeing our countless arguments. I felt a nonverbal resentment from her that the day-to-day sacrifice never allowed her to be anything other than a matronly nonsexual being who lost precious minutes and hours loving her house more than herself.

As I glance at the curtain, I see smeared peanut butter. I realize that I am a mother. Yesterday is gone and all the playacting of childhood could never have prepared me for the real thing. Some authorities believe that the tubes within a newborn's ears are not open. I hope your tubes were open and you heard me say, "I love you, you're my real-live baby doll."

Love, Mom

Self-Help Education: Read SHE 5 on page 88. If you have child(ren), write a paragraph about any guilt you might have about your child(ren) and how their lives are affected by domestic violence. Read SHE 6, page 89.

Dear Son:

There is a mystical cadence as my fingers type feelings back and forth in the form of words. Life gives us so many gifts. It is a beautiful day. As I write to you, I feel like a sculptor who carves thoughts and emotions.

Without a doubt, my relationship with my father was enormously important to help me see clearly. He was the first man I loved and he would be the model for what I would expect from all men. Like many girl children, I lived in a dream world with him.

Right from the start I was taught to please my father. Simultaneously, as he emerged from the interior of his car, the smell of food would come from the kitchen and my mother would yell, "Dad's home, wash the mud pies off the sidewalk."

With every homecoming, I can remember him kneeling, kissing me and whispering, "How's my girl?" His male smell is still vivid to me. I was in awe of him. His uniform, with shiny gold stars across the chest and the bars of a chief petty officer, emphasized his broad shoulders.

We were dependent on him. He was the provider who would bring home pay checks. The house seemed strengthened by his presence. I felt he buffered and protected us from the world. Every time Popeye grabbed his spinach, I was further reinforced that men protected women. My father was my hero.

Marriage to my father made my mother feel more secure from the stresses of this world. I used to go to bed at night wearing a bolt on my ring finger, wishing a prince would enter my dream and carry me off to matrimony. I was a high achiever in school and I poignantly knew how it felt to be torn between being scholastic or popular with boys. I spent a great deal of time in the bathroom meticulously studying magazines that would help make me more salable for marriage.

I felt there was no beginning or end to my father's love. His love propelled me through barriers I once thought had limits. I was an extension of his will. I shadowed my will behind his. I was indulged with spearmint gum, the honor of being the favored daughter, and his compliments. Like a Skinnerian pigeon, his compliments were my pellet reward. When I received a compliment from him, a warm, tingly feeling would pulse throughout my entire body.

He assumed the role of a speech coach who was grooming me to be a lawyer. I entered every speech contest and won money, silver plaques, and engraved pen sets. I felt committed. Winning every speech became a target. I couldn't wait to see him after every glorious victory. Winning a contest was a moment that I wanted to last forever. My father lived vicariously through me.

Making a speech was never a game to me. There was no fun in it. It was the way to get what I wanted: my father's attention. Trying to please him made me incredibly anxious. There seemed to be so many threatening people in the audience staring at me from the safety of their seats. Their simple, aggressive, physical act of staring caused my whole body to tighten. It took time to train myself to look directly at the audience, instead of over their heads, down at the rostrum, or out towards the back of the hall.

My last speech petrified me. To this day, I cannot remember anything from my valedictorian speech other than the white tassel blowing in front of my eyes as I watched the orange sun slowly hide behind the stadium's horizon.

At the awards party afterward, it was humorous to see a boy try to work up enough courage to ask a girl to dance. No one worked up enough courage to ask me. In the ladies' room, the winner turned into the loser, crying in her pink dress. I felt desperate and helpless as I watched the chairs and tables being folded and put away.

I remember being happy as my first love and I chose our gold wedding rings. I also recall that my father died a little and never forgave me when, at twenty, I married my first husband, John.

Our first apartment was an attic above the garage of a house. I loved playing housewife with my two-burner hot plate. I changed my major from Political Science to Home Economics. My father was further devastated.

John was the standby of my youth. My marriage disappointed my father and he pulled away from me emotionally for five years. Increasingly I became unhappy within the confines of a marriage that was too difficult for me to handle. I knew it would never last when I realized that I had the mind of a child at twenty-five. I agonized as I decided to get a divorce.

I wasn't prepared. At the side of my father's bed was a machine that looked like it was a part of a spaceship. The machine's tubes were no longer taped to his arm. He looked so small and was as white as the hospital blanket. My throat ached and I said, "Daddy." I wanted to kiss him but I didn't know if it was all right.

My mind still does not want to remember when without warning, my father's seemingly immovable life was jarred and shaken by the seismographic force of death. His death from lung cancer at fifty-three happened too soon. Meaning trips lightly over this page as I realize that the cleft of time cannot be recrossed. There were so many things he left unfinished. He hadn't retired yet and there were so many ways I would have liked to have known him more deeply. He never really shared his emotions.

Gone are the days when Dinah Shore threw kisses to millions of Americans. My world widened and my personality no longer was shaped by two sincere, fumbling authorities.

Love, Mom

Self-Help Education: Read SHE 7 on page 91. Think about items that you would like to take if you had to leave. Write a brief paragraph about your parents. Include how they talked to you. Mention how anger was handled by your parents. Were you allowed to have your own opinions and express them?

Letter Seven

Dear Son:

As I screamed, I noticed a bad taste coming from my stale smelling mouth. I had to take seriously the threat of him killing me, so I straightened my neck and stared into his eyes. Suddenly my mind snapped and detached itself from its surroundings. My body no longer struggled...I was past caring.

Today, writing would be easier if I could orchestrate my thoughts. I have flashbacks of a prior Hades. More and more of the events that transpired that night are making my stomach churn in revulsion. It's important to understand what happened because battering is such a scarlet letter on my soul. The insult of being beaten scarred my brain more than any demon, any power, a rusty tetanus nail, war. I hated the insult of being beaten like a dog.

My son, sometimes when we sit in the sun with our bottoms on the chilly sidewalk, I try so hard to send thoughts to you. You are so patient. You understand everything I want to relate. You have been my key to growth. I want so much to share that feeling with you. We can't talk yet, you and I. At this moment in time, you are approaching nineteen months. Our verbal conversations consist of all the words you know: "yeah, mama, here, good-bye, hi, doggie, boo, no, see."

There is so much behind my forehead. It takes courage to reveal all the feelings, especially the ones that strike out at me and make me relive pain. There are so many memories that have the morbid smell of threatening death. D-E-A-T-H is a sequence of five letters that is fixed in my mind and is so familiar to me. I have experienced the death of a man who was close to me. He didn't die in the gruesome sickroom of a hospital. This man was never buried and the funeral industry never made a profit from a casket sale. He is your father. He is still living and yet I feel like a widow who is alone, empty, and abandoned. The yearning comes again and again, like waves breaking upon a reef. There is such fierce desire to feel his touch just once more. Because of fate on that night, I have made a decision to mourn him.

You were not physically abandoned by your father. I hope your world is not haunted by your loss of him. I cannot shield you from the pain you will experience from the loss of not sharing your lives together. I do not want the truth to be hidden from you.

For the rest of my life I realize that I cannot contact him. I wouldn't know how to talk to a dead man. In my mind his eyes are glazed with the look of death. The Cold Duck has lost its fizz. It's over. All hope is gone. It's over.

Love, Mom

Self-Help Education: Read SHE 8 on page 93. If you feel your rights have been violated in your relationship, write a brief paragraph pinpointing how they have been violated.

Dear Son:

Splashing in the ocean or walking up a mountain-side seems like a delightful respite from folding pajamas, sweeping up graham cracker crumbs, or hearing the vaporizer hum. I wish I could pick daisies. Where is a large dandelion for my lips to blow?

Sometimes I feel being a single mother is like a debilitating disease that strips me of my independence. I feel trapped. I haven't left the house for three days. Fantasy is the hope that penetrates and rescues my day.

I've found a beautiful gift I would never have dreamed existed. I spend so much time here behind a pane of glass that lets me see the sky. Sometimes the cloud patterns resemble white divinity candy or the soft cheeks of a baby's bottom.

My son, your father is the undercurrent in all my mind's conscious flow...I still love him in so many ways...in crowds or here alone. Uncharted minutes that turn into hours are spent thinking about a love that once was like the safe rooms of childhood. Today, like the quiet presence of reflected light, I saw a cloud-like image that reminded me of him with his boyish Little League grin. He brought out the mother in me.

Just before I met your father, I had turned twenty-eight. I lived in a singles apartment complex and many of the windows were decorated with lots of young plants in macramé hangers. The average tenant stayed six months. The old tenants left without saying good-bye and the new ones installed stereos and wind chimes.

By day I was an elementary school teacher. And, at night in singles bars, sitting on a bar stool and sipping wine, I scouted and preened for "Mr. Right." It took me about an hour to blow dry my hair and select a casual but stylish outfit for the evening. Because I spent so much time trying to look great, I barely managed to wash dishes. Once I let the dishes sit for three days and hurriedly shoved them, dirty, into the oven.

Gradually, I embarked on a frantic round of sexual explorations. Sometimes there was wonderful and truthful communication followed by a believable promise, and then I would never see the person again. Some encounters started with infatuation and then suddenly turned into aversion. On occasion, a few would last more than two weeks. Meaningless sex led me down into a life of a thousand spinning jacks. It proved to be maddening and the love of my life was nowhere in sight.

One morning as I woke up and found last night's disco dress on the floor and another faceless body lying next to me, I found myself thinking, "This can't be me! I can't believe I'm actually doing this to myself." I left that lifestyle behind when I realized that I had the desolate and empty life of a travelling salesman. I got tired of writing my name and phone number on cocktail napkins.

Love, Mom

Self-Help Education: Read SHE 9 on page 95. What characteristics can you identify in your partner?

Letter Nine

Dear Son:

He came to me in a place I never thought I'd meet anyone who would be significant in my life. It started out so simply and unexpectedly. I can still remember the smell of the much-used books and chalk dust.

I noticed a sense of excitement as my kindergartners responded to the morning question: "What would you do with a mountain of ice cream?" That question led the class into a long and marvelous discussion that was interrupted by my principal. "Excuse me, this is Mr. Layton, and I have admitted his daughter Jeneen to your class."

Attraction seems truly to be a multidisciplinary event. And, right from the start, I knew that I was attracted to Mr. Layton. Greg. I liked the way he parted his hair: right down the middle.

When he talked to his daughter, his voice exposed a gentle love. I watched her eyelashes flutter and around her mouth broke a soft smile as he tenderly patted her golden blond hair and said, "I'll be right here to pick you up. I promise. I love you."

You could sense that he was in the emotional process of learning to trust again after a massive,

crippling experience. He had just been scorched by
a separation from his wife, and he carried the weight
of a bad conscience. His wife lived two states away
and ached not knowing where her daughter was.
Jeneen was the main component of a hostile and
complicated child custody suit. Greg had kidnapped
his daughter.

When I met Greg, he was essentially single and
available. Like a classic old movie, I love to rerun
how his eyes seemed to dance when he first asked
me for a date. I noticed a vitality about him when
he spoke, a vitality that reached out and touched
me when I met his eyes. "Can teachers go out on
dates?" he said matter-of-factly.

"Mr. Layton, for God's sake, I can't go out with
my student's father! What do you want from me?"

"Everything," he said quietly, "I want you."

I agreed to cook a dinner if he bought the food.

I put so much expectation into that first date.
That afternoon, I tried to straighten up the house. I
washed a two-week accumulation of dirty clothes
and even cleaned the gray ring in the bathroom sink.
And just in case, I took the cookie-crumbed sheets
off the bed and put clean ones on.

"You look great," he said as he handed me the
bag of food and a bottle of Cold Duck. I felt uneasy
as I silently poured the Cold Duck into two jelly

glasses. The room seemed dreadfully silent so I put on a neutral jazz record. When I handed him his glass, he looked so handsome. I hoped he wouldn't notice that I studied his body the way a child might memorize his mother's face.

As the night and the conversation proceeded, he seemed like a rare magnet that increasingly pulled me into orbit. "I really enjoyed the dinner. It was fantastic. May I come back?" he said with so much appreciation.

As I nodded I replied, "I love to cook, especially when it's appreciated." I had never met anyone like him and felt slighted when he kissed me without passion and left at eleven o'clock.

After a couple of dates, our feelings for each other grew. One night, something occurred that took us both so unaware. We were a little frightened as we got caught in the vortex of something that seemed to make the universe hold its breath. We sat opposite each other and deliberately held a continuous smile as if we had known each other forever. As we swirled and fell endlessly, a silent laughter shimmered throughout our bodies and communication commenced without the need to verbalize or gesture. We had no idea where all this would lead us when we walked to the bedroom without discussion.

I remember a growing urgency as we silently undressed. The room seemed to explode into a delirious primitive ecstasy as we made love several times under and over the sheets. Toward the end of the night, we exchanged the magic words, "I love you." I was awakened that night by the confusing and insistent noise of a candle burning low. As I noticed my dry lips, he leaned over and kissed my cheek, "Go back to sleep, my love." Obediently, I closed my eyes and asked myself, "Could this be Prince Charming?"

It was as if this were all happening to someone else. I spent the next weeks in a state of euphoria. I thought I would go out of my mind until I would see him again. The minutes stubbornly refused to move.

Within no time the kindergarten teacher was living with Mr. Layton and his daughter, Jeneen. It was not dirty or sordid. I slept with the man I loved and had parachuted into a new life.

For me, the best invitation to child's play was when he stepped bare-bellied out of the shower. A sudden spontaneous giddiness would come over me and without warning I'd throw my arms around him and knock him off balance. As I ran down the hall, I'd tantalize him in a juvenile tone, "Make love to me first."

Happiness was lying in bed together.

I centered my life waiting in happiness for him to come home so we could have supper together.

Our favorite entree was mushrooms sautéed in butter. His stories were so fascinating. He was an antique dealer who would talk with so much enthusiasm about this deal and that one. As we talked, my mind would release memories and anecdotes that I had saved just for him. Our conversations were fascinating and intense. We felt related in a secret way and listened endlessly to each other as we unraveled the threads of our lives. We told each other everything.

He seemed so strong. Endlessly, he would listen to me with a devotion as strong as tempered steel. When I talked he would lean toward me and fix his incredible brown eyes on mine. At the risk of being shattered by a careless remark, I let him enter the far reaches of my soul. I found myself telling him intricate parts of my dreams. Without any fear I told him about my previous sex life. He told me about his wife.

My mask of structured defenses collapsed and my usual sharp judgment turned into a soft, pink focus. I didn't pay attention to the clues. He did not come to me with a resume of his past emotional history.

One Saturday morning, we were startled by the insistent and demanding ring of the telephone. In my twilight sleep as I pulled the covers over my head, I noticed that his voice was furious. I gathered that he was talking to his wife, Sarah.

"I'm not ever going to let you see her again! Look what you did to me, you bitch! You robbed me of everything and destroyed my world. I gave you all my love." His voice pierced my eardrum. "You took and took, you bitch."

I had never heard his voice so angry, so frightening. I tried hiding myself deeper underneath the blanket. I didn't want to hear any part of that conversation. As I got up to go to the bathroom, I remember him sitting on the side of the bed with an ugly scowl on his face. He was listening to her and then suddenly without warning, he yanked the phone out of the wall and threw it across the room. The silence in the room was deafening. I had never seen such a display of anger.

I was apprehensive when I gave him a cup of coffee and said, "What was that all about?" He looked like one big tear drop. His hands fumbled as he lit a cigarette.

"She's found me and says the court has ordered me to give Jeneen back. I'll never see my daughter again." And then suddenly like a flash flood his voice got louder as so many bottled feelings came out. "There wasn't enough money. She never thought I made enough money. I tried so hard to please her." He started to yell and cry as he slammed the coffee cup on the night stand. "You have no idea what it's like to take care of a wife and kid. And then she had to leave and take Jeneen with her. That ungrateful bitch. Sometimes I worry about you. You really don't know what happened."

In a puzzled tone I asked, "What do you mean?" He never replied and laid his head in my lap.

We had our secrets, Greg and I. In the days and weeks that followed, any dark memory that surfaced in his brain led him back to a past solitary and painful expedition: his unresolved relationship with his wife. He became distant and we no longer had our marathon sharing sessions. When Jeneen returned to her mother, I found myself consoling a man whom I had thought was unwavering. He didn't seem to care; it was as if someone had injected a big syringe of novocaine into his brain.

He tried to re-invest his feelings in me. He never fully understood the mechanics of the failure in his marriage. We were doomed to make the same mistakes. I failed to heed the hostile feeling he had toward his wife and his inability to see his contribution to the breakup of his marriage. Kidnapping Jeneen from his wife was a tactical maneuver in a marriage that had turned into a mine field.

Love, Mom

> **Self-Help Education:** Read SHE 10 on page 98. Can you pinpoint how you might send out signals that you are a victim? What do you say or do?

Dear Son:

Today, the memories of what we once shared
have hit me with the force of a cannonball. I
am consciously blinking back an unexpected on-
slaught of tears.

I loved him. I always meant to be there. I was
committed to him even if I didn't have a wedding
band. I wanted to understand him like a course in
chemistry.

After Jeneen left our lives, his dreams seemed to
burst like pricked balloons...one right after another.
His antique business wasn't working out financially.

Something else added stress to our lives and I
remember celebrating the event without any consid-
eration to practicality. I looked closely at my stomach to see a bulge. Tiny hands and feet weren't a
reality yet. You were just a round mass of cells that
must have looked like a cluster of minute bubbles.
Your beginning was a glorious secret that I wanted
so much to share with your father. You are the root
of our relationship.

"Greg?" "Yeah," he replied without looking away
from the television. "I've got something to tell you,
please listen."

"All right, I'm listening. Come sit by me." He guided me to the armchair and we both sat a little sideways so we could fit. Without a preamble, I blurted out, "I'm pregnant."

His reaction wasn't exactly what I had expected from the short stories about motherhood in *McCall's*. I still remember the blast of his breath on my face, "Bitch." For an eternity, he remained wordlessly silent. He didn't even look at me. I could have been a blip on a radar screen. Finally, I watched his lips press together and form words that echoed with anger. "What do you mean? Whose baby is it? You whore. You slut. It's not my baby." I felt paralyzed. Without letting me answer, he rose quickly and threw a newspaper at me. The pages fluttered before my eyes. The tension was unbearable. I left the room feeling the highest distrust. If I could have been granted one wish, it would have been to die instantly. I couldn't cry. I felt nothing. Nothing! I felt betrayed and rejected with my most supreme present. He was right there when we played "baby maybe." We both knew the consequences of using no contraceptives.

As I hurriedly packed, his voice filled me with tenderness. "Please, you're all I've got left. I love you." I overlooked the awful words he had just spoken. We became friends again right there by the suitcases.

He made love to me so tenderly. I couldn't remember just when the last time had been. When he started to kiss me, my whole body felt like liquid. He knew all the right things to do for hours and hours.

The next day, as a peace offering, I was given yellow daisies and a chocolate sweetheart. I couldn't stay mad at him. Part of me felt anger and hatred and the other part remembered our love. I was confused and started to doubt my conflicting emotions. I started doubting myself.

Love, Mom

Self-Help Education: What do you like about yourself? Can you think of three things that you do well?

Letter Eleven

Dear Son:

If someone had taken a picture of us, we would have been appropriate for a Hallmark congratulations card. Your father and I were proud when you were born. Tears flowed from our eyes.

Day after day in the hospital, your father and I visited your bassinet. In our eyes you made no trivial movements. We watched your head turn and follow your Dad's finger. We talked to you, made funny faces, and gently rattled paper to amuse you. Your little china-blue eyes seemed to always be asking where you were and why.

With your birth, a definite change took place in my life. Bang! My old life was over when we brought you home and laid you in your crib.

I find it difficult to relate the enormity of my feelings when I began my role as a mother. I couldn't move my thoughts past better-check-to-see-if-you're breathing, your bowel movements, or your colic.

I wish I could say our feedings looked like a Madonna-and-child painting. My breasts were so full of milk. They looked like plump casaba melons. They burned and ached. I remember sitting with you in my arms during those late night feedings. I felt so inadequate as you screamed from colic in my arms. Sometimes, I could do nothing to abate your incessant crying. Often, we both ended up crying. In my innocence and exhaustion, I told myself that someday things would get back to normal. I felt stuck within the grooves of a tedious routine that seemed like an ever-repeating record.

I can't say I was committed to you from the beginning. I envisioned the experience to be something like a glorious journey terminating with congratulations and cheering for my successful mothering...sort of like winning Wimbledon or the New York lottery. The plan was to let you be your own person, to make all your baby food, breast feed, and never sit you down in front of the TV. That was the original plan. I had no notion what motherhood was all about.

For the first nine weeks of your life your tiny body reddened into a ball. Your colic often agitated me and made me nervous and short-tempered. I never knew how much time I had for anything; it was unnerving. I learned to go to the bathroom and take a shower as fast as I could. I felt like a wired machine changing diapers, cutting nails, and washing baby clothes. At the apartment laundromat, I often found myself caught with four baskets of dirty clothes and the wrong change; the change machine usually was out of order. I was staggered by the coin combinations. The washing machines took two quarters and a dime, not six dimes, or twelve nickels.

You were with me constantly. I talked to you often. I didn't venture out of the house because I was so exhausted. For relaxation, I would find a quiet little spot on the couch and listen to music as I fell asleep. I felt a sense of accomplishment if I was dressed before noon.

My life with you was influenced by how I viewed the world. I quickly became absorbed in a whole new way of life called motherhood. I began to notice things that had never caught my attention. Fathers only occasionally changed diapers and rarely gave the "little woman a night out." As far as my attention to him went, your father felt usurped in his position. Oftentimes, the house was a mess. Once he stood in the kitchen and shook his head in despair. "I don't understand why all this baby shit has to be all over the house. I can't get past all these damn baby bottles in the refrigerator!" Tiny, hurt feelings ran loose in my heart.

He did not accept you and soon convinced me that he wanted no more children. I was sterilized two months after you were born. I did not do it willingly: I had always wanted two children.

We both wanted the old maelstrom in which we had once passionately and dizzily whirled to come back. He bought me a bottle of perfume and presented it to me in orange gift wrap with a regal gold bow. I bought him a Moody Blues album. On impulse we decided to go to the ocean. We left you at a babysitter's.

That evening at the ocean, we carefully dressed for our walk on the beach. I wore a soft blue sweater with nothing underneath except perfume. My hair hung around my shoulders and formed a backdrop for my crystal earrings. He wore a bulky turtleneck sweater and a hat that looked like a train conductor's. He looked handsome.

Ironically, the weather that night was unbelievably bleak and amplified the emptiness we felt. Somehow we knew, as we lay there in each other's arms looking at the soft rolling breakers splash along the shore, that all tensions, even parenting, affected our relationship. We didn't speak for a long time. He studied my face seriously and said, "Remember when it was like a fever? Am I mad? We loved each other, didn't we?" I nodded and could see that his face telegraphed fear and worry. Words were meaningless.

I ache sometimes when I am impatient with you. I have been so discouraged and tired. After I have contended with the world another day, I wearily put you in your blue crib with the white lamb painted on its side. I quietly talk to you and ask you to forgive me for my irritations. I want you to wake up and listen to me. I want you to see the anguish as it trickles down my cheek and lands softly on your baby quilt. My God, you are so dependent on me!

It feels uncomfortable to see the reality of you, an extension of myself. Wouldn't it have been better for you to have stayed in the warmth of my womb and bathed in the security of my walls? Wasn't it better to lie peacefully in those waters I made for you, than to swim in this big pool called earth?

Love, Mom

Self-Help Education: Refer to SHE 14 on page 108. How do you handle depression? Write a paragraph about what you tend to do. Do you isolate yourself? Do you eat more? Do you use drugs or alcohol?

Letter Twelve

Dear Son:

The milk was stored in the upper left-hand side of the top shelf in the refrigerator. The toothpaste stayed out on the counter.

We had our rituals.

On Saturdays, we would spend long, leisurely hours in bed reading the newspaper. Sometimes, in bed, we ate chocolate mousse for breakfast. We giggled and felt like naughty little children when we spent the entire morning in bed. On Saturdays the bedroom floor was decorated with newspapers.

We studied gourmet cookbooks and were amazed at our culinary masterpieces. We delighted in inventing some of our own and made up names for them. The one with chicken breasts stuffed with Monterey jack and covered with avocado and wine sauce was the "Good, Good, Chicken Vibration." We washed down many of our concoctions with chilled white wine. Many of our toasts to one another were promises that we would always stay in love.

I can't pinpoint when we were pulled down to earth's level with a vengeance. But life gradually changed into a more strenuous existence as small impediments altered the flow of our feelings. Looking back now, everything seemed to perpetuate the violence: *Gunsmoke*, toy guns, Viet Nam, boxing gloves, Kennedy's assassination. The main triggering ingredient was that we knew each other too well; we were all too aware of each other's vulnerable spots. Unknowingly, our trusting statements became the seeds of our eventual hellish drama. We knew each brick in the other's erected walls of defense.

At first, he didn't put up a good front. I knew that Clark Kent did not live beneath his superman exterior. Everything was not all right. The business had folded and he had to resort to driving a truck. Money became a very scarce commodity in our lives. Unpaid bills set our teeth on edge. Inflation didn't help us either. Rent and groceries took up a great portion of the paycheck.

Increasingly, our lives became separate. He had his work and I had my domestic affairs. He brought home the paychecks, I managed the money and balanced the check book. My identity gradually became blurred and linked to the house. I spent a great deal of time alone and felt restless with my new role. I bought his shirts and ironed them. I bought the groceries and started cooking all the meals. I pretended to not collapse under all my endless chores and maintained a façade of strength. The toilet bowl seemed to have my name on it.

Pressures…pressures…pressures…"We ran out of toilet paper again." "Oh, I thought you were going to buy some on your way home." "I really don't like your friends." "I need money for baby formula." "I can't stand kissing you after you smoke those damn cigarettes. Go brush your teeth." "Why don't you fold the towels differently?" "You really think this is a meal?" The war of the words had started. Only on rare occasions did we look at cookbooks together anymore.

More and more, television became our main form of entertainment. I got tired of sharing him with the networks. The canned laughter and stupid situations were watched during meals, when we had company, and even when we made love. It turned into a habit. Sometimes when I left the room to say "good night" he would respond with a casual remark or answer me with a grunt or a shake of a newspaper. I couldn't help feeling that he was closing me out. He looked more and more doomed as the burdens of family life became a reality.

His verbal abuse was so destructive. It penetrated my self-esteem and wounded my self-confidence. At first, like Tarzan, his angry, verbal assaults seemed powerful and a little exciting. The excitement was short-lived and all too soon, I was confronted with his jealousy. He was jealous of any interaction I had with other men. I had to account for my time. He made me uncomfortable with my old sex life. Sometimes he berated me if I wanted sex. He started hu-

miliating me in public and degraded me in private
by intimating that I was less intelligent than he was.
I kept telling myself to say something in my defense,
but I couldn't speak. I just sat there and stared at
him. Anger was buried so deeply I could feel it
rumbling.

I used sex as a reward for Greg's good behavior.
The system was totally under my control. I would
never tell him in advance the exact behavior that
would beget the reward. I had praised his earlier
sexual participation but now there was no sexual
stimulation or expression of warmth that I ordained
as correct. Increasingly, sex became more and more
disappointing.

I felt turned off by him. His lips felt cold and
hard. When he kissed me, I turned my head away.
I felt hollow and harbored no feelings of sexuality.
I no longer savored the feel of his skin. He didn't
even smell the same. I had great bouts of anxiety
and hated lying next to him in bed.

Our love was tinged with a poignant sadness.
The adoration had disappeared. I no longer was
blind to his faults and weaknesses. He had lost
some of his charm. Sometimes, even after some of
the worst verbal fights, we worked our way back to
each other. But sex was always quite different than
before. It lacked a great deal of its former passion.
There was so much to ignore and so much to forget; I took deep breaths sometimes to get through

it. Our bedtime conversations no longer had any gaiety in them. So much dangerous terrain had finally affected our loving and nothing would feel as sweet as it had before.

My mind is awash with so many memories. I can remember when the physical violence started to happen. I can recall an incident that made me want to wipe tabasco in his eyes. If I could have, I would have stuffed dry spaghetti down his throat. There was so much mental havoc caused by the lack of peace between your father and me. I can't keep denying that I wasn't a part of the beginning of our domestic violence. But I can say without hesitation that I did not deserve to be beaten. I could have been killed when my neck was shoved backwards. He had no right to act out his anger on my body.

As I write, my feet feel like they are on familiar ground. I can see vividly what happened and feel that I am back in time. His image is so clear to me. As I began to get out of bed he suddenly became furious. I can almost hear his voice. It sounded like thunder. "Lay with me, what's the matter?"

"I can't, Greg. I feel a little anxious about something. I don't want to disturb you. I'll sleep on the couch. Go to sleep." He jumped up and started shouting at me, "You're withholding sex from me to punish me and now you won't even sleep with me. You damn slut."

I threw my legs over the side of the bed and curled a lock of hair around my index finger and sneered at him with a sinister and totally artificial smile. I hated being barked at like that and fought back with all the verbal ammo I could muster. In an ironic and sarcastic voice I blurted out, "You bastard, now I understand why she left you. You treated her like a piece of shit!"

As I stood up, he grabbed my nightgown and I lost my balance. I fell backward and quickly lunged toward the seeming security of a closet. It wasn't a haven. I saw the kick come and shifted my body to take it on my back. My back felt a fiery, deep pain that I cannot even communicate. My vision blurred. As I got up, my legs seemed to buckle and my eyes were blinded by tears. As I staggered into the bathroom, I felt cold and numb. When he raced after me, I drew back. I'm sure my eyes were wild with fright. He shook his head and shocked me with his intense apologetic repentance, "God, don't let this be the end. I'm sorry! I didn't mean to hurt you." I had never seen a man beg before. I felt vaguely powerful and forgave him.

I didn't sleep that night. I lay there with my hands folded on my breasts. My breathing was different. It seemed so internal. I thought I had died and been reborn when the sun came through the curtains. I just lay there in bed as my eyes stared at the ceiling. I turned my head and saw his face…a face whose lips had once kissed me. His face appeared to me like a *Samurai* sword, piercing my stomach. His whole body appeared lifeless, cold, like a wax figure.

Love, Mom

Self-Help Education: Read SHE 13 on page 106. Refer to SHE 12 on page 103 and put a paper alongside this questionnaire. Where do you stand?

Dear Son:

It would have taken a miracle like Moses parting the sea for him to quit beating me. We both had become triggers. I berated him if his paychecks weren't enough or if he failed to put his underwear in the dirty clothes hamper. Once a fight started because he found that I had put two butter dishes in the refrigerator.

In my eyes he was the enemy, my opponent. I treated him in a cold, businesslike manner, not warm, not even lukewarm. The flow between our shores slowly closed. There was an atmosphere of war. Life had squeezed our two wills together and formed an explosive friction. To see who was stronger, we crushed each other's will by condescending to one another.

Physical violence happened again and again. He was always able to physically overtake me, he was stronger. My prowess was verbal: I became adept at verbally aggravating him. I knew exactly how to ride him. After our fights, there was always a cycle of hurt and healing. We both felt pain. For both of us, making up afterward wasn't always easy. I would emotionally turn off and would act like he didn't exist. The muscles in my cheeks did not work; my lips did not smile. When he hit me he felt humiliated. He abhorred the fact that he had hit me and made so many peace offerings. It was hard to accept any of them because my brain had so many unpleasant thoughts boring through it. He had started to look more like a demon than a demigod. He had lost so much respect in my eyes that it was difficult to look into his. Jean Naté bubble baths didn't help. Nothing helped. We both suffered.

I felt separated from every other person and thing in God's creation. I called my family less frequently. When I did call, I tried very hard to conceal what was going on. Except for trips to have group counseling and hear the hang-ups of a half-dozen other poor souls, I lived alone in a desperate and terrifying existence. I saw no way to change it.

I bought makeup to disguise the bruises on my face and body. As I dabbed foundation under my eyes, I kept silently telling myself that my life was perfect...perfect. I became compulsive. I couldn't go to sleep at night until the sink was dry of every last drop of water. My friends told me that my voice changed; they said that I spoke rapidly and went off on tangents. I went to a doctor who gave me little pills to help me relax. A clergyman told me that I should go home and be more tolerant. I felt I was trapped in a tiger's cage and didn't know where to go with my anxiety.

All doors to interaction with other people were slowly barred when he felt that my friends and family were a threat to our relationship. I became terrified and learned to realize a fear that harbored itself in every tissue, bone, vein, muscle, and nerve of my body. When I stared at a face in the mirror that I no longer knew, my hands trembled with fright. I could hardly control them to put on lipstick. I did not know who I was anymore. I felt like my body was composed of a million molecules and all of them were disintegrating at once. I tried to deny everything that was happening. Most of the time, I convinced myself that your father and I lived in a glorious and peaceful cocoon. I glorified him to anyone who would listen. But a section of my brain felt a helpless hatred toward him that went through my brain like little jolts of electricity. Often, I found myself twisting a ring that he had given me back and forth around my finger. It seemed like a talisman of evil, an artifact that reminded me of his betrayal.

My security became living the way he wished. I was obedient and lost my will to take a chance at the unknown. One night in the shower, I tried to figure out something I could do, someplace I could go. I came up with nothing. The life I had was familiar, even with its terror. I kept on thinking that he was your father and that you should be raised by two parents. I felt helpless and was economically dependent. My only skill was teaching kindergarten. In California, at that time, the only available teaching jobs were in private schools. I knew I could not support you and me on a private school teacher's salary. My only other resort was to go on welfare, an idea I abhorred. With all the power within me, I tried to visualize hope. I hoped that the beatings would stop. I felt so guilty for being unhappy.

The last battle was different from all the rest. I still can hear the sound of war pounding in my brain. To this day, I feel disgust and horror from a dream being crushed before my eyes: my family.

Love, Mom

Self-Help Education: Re-read SHE 14 on page 108. Do you think you are in a depression? Write a brief paragraph about what you are now feeling. Do you have any symptoms of depression?

Letter Fourteen

Dear Son:

This letter is so hard to write. I am afraid to look back. I wish I could distort so many of the details of that night. But I realize that I can't change the pattern of a snowflake or what happened. It was a night of immense tension. A trusted friend has taken you to a park.

Your father and I lived together twenty months and twenty-one days. I have to go so far behind the mirror of time.

He was no longer driving a truck. He sold refrigerators on commission. We lived from paycheck to paycheck. It was always difficult to pay the rent. When the California court system allowed us to see Jeneen, we thought we would sacrifice anything to see her again. Her plane ticket was very expensive; the cost of the ticket had come out of our living expenses. She stayed with us for two weeks. Money became even more scarce; we ate a lot of burritos.

In the morning as I cleared away the breakfast dishes, I glanced at the beams of sunlight as they danced through the window above the sink. I knew the temperature would be well over 100 degrees. It was a Sunday morning in July...July 21, 1979.

To other people in the neighborhood we might have looked like the golden couple: young, strong new parents. Our appearance to the world, however, was very deceiving.

I was tired of my position as the battered domestic technician. I was tired of doing all the housework, all the banking, and all of the parenting. I could not take the beatings anymore. That day I realized that I had come to my breaking point: black became white. I felt so incredibly weary and thought I had no life left.

I feel I can breathe easier as I start to remember more of the events that led up to that night. You spent a great deal of the day in a playpen on the front porch. I washed a lot of clothes and recall hating to hang them up on the clothesline. There were so many of them. Jeneen lost her tooth that day and we celebrated with a tea party. One of her friends from across the street brought over warm muffins and joined us.

That night, I made a special good-bye dinner for Jeneen. She was going back to her mother the next day: the two week stay was nearly at an end. Unexpectedly, Greg called to say that he would be thirty minutes late. The hours rolled by. I had to make so many apologies to his daughter. I kept telling her, "Your Dad will be here soon. You'll see. He wouldn't miss this night."

He was several hours late, and walked through the door slightly drunk holding a beer in his hand. I sat on the edge of the couch and made a speech I'd been rehearsing over and over in my head. "I've had it with this house! I've had it with you! You can take care of the kids! I need to go out and have some fun!" And then I said something I knew would make him mad, "I want to go to a bar and have a drink!" I grabbed the keys and walked swiftly to the car. I thought he was going to rip off the car door. He yanked me out of the car and talked to me with a shocking harshness, "You damn slut. Where do you think you're going?"

"I told you that I want to go to a bar. I want to have fun like you do after work. Do you think it's fun to be here all day without a car and wait on two kids and then wait on you at night? I don't even feel appreciated anymore!" The violent volcano of protest inside of me had finally exploded: the anger inside me had erupted like hot lava.

All hell broke loose. His eyes spoke a language I couldn't recognize: they were full of a deadly rage. I can still see him rolling up his shirt sleeves and flinging up the hood of the car. He ripped out the spark plug wires and threatened to whip my face by thrusting his clenched fist under my nose. I began to cry frantically. "Oh, God, please no!" As I ran toward the house, he gripped my arm. I tried to cover my head with both of my hands. I was defenseless. My left hand and left side of my face were whipped and stung from the spark plug wires. He pushed me down against the sidewalk and pulled my hair and shoved my neck backwards. My eyes burned as he methodically drizzled the rest of his beer in my eyes.

The night before I had not been able to sleep after a nightmare that left my body wet and shivering. I wrestled with him as hard as I could, but I was weak from lack of sleep. He was too strong for me. At one point I got up and ran into the house and tried hiding underneath the kitchen table. Except for when my father had died, I had never felt so terrible. The tears ran down my cheeks. My whole body felt hollow and helpless. The pain felt like it was eating out my bones. I felt like I was in a trance as I concentrated on my breathing. My chest seemed to bellow. My mind screamed in pain when my eye transmitted the most frightening sight. I saw his clenched fist with his black onyx ring come toward my jaw. Inside my head I heard a cracking sound. My hearing changed markedly: everything sounded as if I was under water. Blood trickled out of my mouth. I felt very faint and wanted to get out of the house. I thought I would be safer outside in the neighborhood. When I stepped through the screen door, I felt like I was the next person in line for a painful vaccination: my neighbors had gathered outside to watch the fight. I found that old feeling of humiliation had come back, but this time my private space was really being violated. I had cherished my privacy but now we were the entertainment for the entire neighborhood. The neighborhood looked on and did not intervene when I yelled out, "Please help me!" We were photographed with their eyes. The world seemed so cold and inanimate.

I was beaten up on my front lawn on and off for the next two or three hours. I experienced everything from a distance, as if it were not happening to me. I felt as if someone had touched the back of my neck with a cattle prod when he yelled out, "I never wanted that blasted kid!" I tried to yell for help but my words lacked volume. My words could not flow from my mouth. My body was tremendously weak from the tension and stress. The tone of my voice cracked and my tongue tasted like cardboard. My body shook uncontrollably.

His forehead was pinched together in a frown. The corners of his mouth exposed his teeth. His eyes were fixed on me. My arms and heart burned. Without any warning he kicked me and threw me across the grass. I fell and plunged to the ground. He kicked me in my stomach and lower right kidney. As he shook and pounded my head against the grass, my arms were held down. My neck felt like a rubber band as he screamed and yelled in my face: his saliva sprayed all over my face. The veins in his neck bulged and his face was white as he uttered, "If you don't admit to this neighborhood that you have been stealing my money and going out with other men, I'll bash your head like an egg on this sidewalk. Understand?"

I nodded and quietly said, "Yes, you're right." I wanted to survive. At that point a hollow voice surfaced within me, "Is this really the way my life will end? Is death the only rational exit? Where are the police and why won't someone help me?" I could feel panic surging throughout my body. I took several breaths to try to calm down.

"Louder, you damn bitch. You're just like Sarah. You know you've screwed other guys behind my back!"

In a zombie-like voice, I uttered, "You're right. I'm just like her." I knew his mind had snapped and that I had better say what he wanted even if I had always been faithful. My heart was beating so fast. I felt like I was being shaken by a bear and at any moment my skull was about to be crushed. With my whole body I assumed a submissive posture to help communicate that I conceded defeat. My head was lowered and I held my hands together.

Like a miracle, something happened that saved my life. He stubbed out his last cigarette. As he left, he said, "I'm going to the store to get another pack of cigarettes. If you leave, I'll track you down and kill you."

I could barely hear myself for the noise of my heart. "OK."

After he left, I felt so exposed. My dress was ripped and my arms had bruises on them. My fingers had blood all over them. My whole body ached when I walked to the door and closed it. I went through the house and turned all the lights on. Jeneen was huddled on her bed. She was in shock. I was afraid that he would come back and tear my limbs off. A massive wave of panic went through my body. And then suddenly, three neighbors walked in unannounced. As one of them washed my face and gave me a Valium, the other neighbor said, "You have to get out of here now! He'll be back soon. You won't be safe here. There is a shelter for women like you!"

"What do you mean, 'women like me'?"

"We've been hearing it for months. Your fights are quite loud. You're a battered woman."

I picked you up from your baby crib, put a sweater on Jeneen, got my purse, and one baby bottle. We left behind all that was familiar...the chairs, baby clothes, my clothes, photographs, sewing machine, and a life of terror.

Love, Mom

Self-Help Education: Read SHE 11 on page 101.

Dear Son:

The apartment is so silent. You are asleep.

In these final words I will not offer polished phrases or delicately molded clauses. I cannot refine the contents of these letters into dry theories.

My battering is in the past. Writing to you was a valid pathway that led me to transformation and inner peace. I am convinced that I am recovering from the experience of battering and know that I will become a stronger, surer woman. Lately, with each struggle, with each anxiety and frustration and with each new decision that I have had to make, I am regaining more of my self-confidence. No part of this process has been easy. I am in the process of building a new life, brick by brick.

Even though my battering is a historical fact in my life, I am aware of mental scar tissue that is faintly tender to the touch. It would be less than honest to say that my "Alice-Down-the-Rabbit-Hole" way of life did not affect me physically and mentally.

My hearing is impaired and I still have not regained the ability to fully taste food: the taste buds on the left side of my tongue are irrevocably damaged. My jaw pops when I eat.

After my abuse there still seemed to be shrapnel lodged in my brain. Feeling hopeless, I experienced some of the darkest days of my life. Sometimes I still feel pieces of shrapnel but increasingly I am feeling a contentment that cannot even be hinted at in words.

Writing to you has helped me to face how people deal with battering. They deal with it as something just a bit too threatening to be admitted in daily discourse. Almost everyone deals with the subject nervously.

My mother saw my abuse as one of her own failures. I distinctly remember her questioning me on the Christmas Eve after my battering: "How could you have done this to our family? How did you let it happen?" Her face looked so angry and disappointed.

On another occasion I felt even more isolated. My sister called me one day and without explanation said that she and her new husband could no longer be godparents to you. Fear had surrounded any association with us.

The vulnerability I felt after being battered was often a very lonely experience. People who knew about the abuse I received treated me gingerly. One day I opened the phone directory and began to flip through it. I hoped that I would find the name of someone to call. I found no one. When friends did call me they sounded distant, and cold. It was very difficult to firm up any social get-togethers with them. Their calls were polite and brief. They didn't want to be involved with me. They were just checking in to see if I was still alive. My battering was painfully obvious to me and the people who knew me. I was overcome by waves of depression when I realized that I was no longer accepted as a part of the human race. I felt emotionally disgraced and banished to a solitary life. The black clouds in my life started to dissipate when I realized that this society didn't have to change; I needed to change my thinking about abuse.

I am learning to drop all pretensions about battering. Increasingly, I seem to be able to drop the false façade that my life is perfect and have started talking openly about my experience. To my surprise, I no longer feel like the only passenger on an excursion boat out of hell.

I am starting to meet women who have waited to find someone who would listen to them without judgment. Their horror stories seem to always spill out in torrents of relief. Their testimonials are helping me restore my sense of self. I feel a kinship toward these women who have divulged their daily fears.

The woman who made me feel like a true comrade was Sarah, Greg's former wife. While I was in the shelter, I called her to see if Jeneen had gotten back safely. Sarah said Jeneen was with her and was safe. During the course of our conversation, Sarah said softly, "Honey, you're not Greg's first victim. I left with Jeneen and all my belongings because I got tired of the holes in the walls, the hospital emergency rooms, and the police reports. I got tired of the fear."

Other battered women have helped me out of my feelings of isolation. It helps to have their support because nearly everyone else associates a "battered woman" with a lost, unredeemable segment of society. Some of my best friends have admitted to their beating. One friend confided that she had been "psychologically" battered and exposed a scar that had lacerated her mind. I have doubts if she will ever again have self-confidence or trust.

Like so many other women, I was battered while still believing that it couldn't happen to me. It has taken me a while to understand what really happened to Greg and me. Because of that night, I am convinced that our fates will always be inextricably entangled.

For a long time, I associated everything in my world with Greg. The thought of Greg was painful like an open wound. I would wonder where he was, what he was doing...who he was with or doing it to. I felt furious and outraged that a man could have violated me both physically and spiritually. I stereotyped all men as the only ingredient in a domestic

violence situation. One day, when I was in a grocery
store I saw a young male clerk get furious when a
whole mountain of cheese fell from a display. An ex-
hibition of anger by a man made me afraid. I clearly
had a problem with anything that even merely re-
sembled that night. I had to walk out of the store.
After that incident, I found that I truly needed to understand the conflict between Greg and me. The
myriad of conflicting emotions I had toward men
consumed me.

Writing to you has helped me stop kidding myself. I have learned to stop blaming him and have
started facing the truth about myself. My ego was
threatened and challenged when I realized that I
was a verbal master in knowing how to aggravate
Greg. He used a weapon, however, that I couldn't
compete with: his physical strength.

Your father and I were in darkness because of
our ignorance about handling our anger. As we
went through life there was no harmony: we hit all
the wrong notes. I do believe that both Greg and I
lived in a world that predisposed us to the violence.
There is no one, however, that I can point to with a
self-righteous finger as the culprit. The explorations
of our childhood might seem trivial, but in retrospect
the messages of both of our youths kept us locked
in a daily torment. In our childhood, we never
learned how to deal with our anger. He was taught
to act it out with his body. In my childhood, anger
was something to be hidden and covered up. And

now, we both carry our stigmas: he is a batterer and I am a battered woman. We both have suffered. However, his inability to deal with problems other than by violent confrontations was a complete denial of my rights as a human being. I strongly believe that no one deserves to be beaten.

X Anger is natural. It is a simple reality in this world. How we view anger and approach our differences is paramount. My association with other women is helping me to understand something monumental. Some women are guilty of verbally aggravating their own battering. And some women are innocent of perpetrating their abuse. I truly believe that an understanding of ourselves as women involved with men in the stress and strain of this century is paramount. To stop the vicious cycle, we must understand the evolution of battering. In order to release ourselves from being battered, knowledge of abuse must be balanced. Men are not the only villains. X

I believe that both men and women were meant to say a vibrant "yes" to the full human experience. The differences between men and women are only superficial: there are so many countless ways we are alike. Both men and women can be freed from the vicious cycle of abuse when our inward thoughts have changed in how we perceive anger.

I look upon myself as a young woman who carries something simple in my heart: battering renders both sexes unfit to enjoy God's gift of life. The long-playing battle of the sexes must end, or our species will annihilate itself from within its most important building block: the family.

During these letters, I have always felt that I was being led by an inner prompting to record what we have been through before it was altered and changed by the distance of time. Many times, I felt the ache of being afraid to reveal myself for fear of losing you. Often, it would drift through my mind that one day you would reject me. As I write, I have a big lump in my throat. The pressure is so hard to bear. There is still a fear of being left alone after I have revealed too much of myself to you. Writing to you helped me climb the highest mountain and helped me to understand what happened. I hope these letters will also help you to understand the truth. Years from now, I will not give them to you as the act of the ultimate, martyr mother. I hope they will keep you from being caught in the vicious web of domestic violence.

Your father and I loved each other...we once traded our hearts. Neither of us wanted the final door to slam and force our lives into two separate existences. The crux of it all is that we both did not understand our anger.

As I come to a close, I feel so relieved. The room suddenly seems to be getting brighter. I can breathe again. I want to turn the volume up on the record player. I want it to seem like there is a crowd in this room. I am alive!

Love, Mom

Self-Help Education: If you have been a victim of domestic violence, write this sentence ten times: "I deserve respect."

National Statistics on Domestic Violence

• In 1985, over 1,300 women were killed by a husband or boyfriend, which was 30 percent of the total homicides of females; six percent of the male victims of homicide were killed by their wives or girlfriends.
(Federal Bureau of Investigation. (1986). *Uniform Crime Reports: Crime in the United States,* 1985. Washington, DC: U.S. Department of Justice)

• Approximately 37 percent of pregnant patients, across class, race, and educational lines, are physically abused.
(Helton A, McFarlane J, Anderson E. Battered and pregnant: a prevalence study. *Am J Public Health.* 1987: 77: 1337-1339)

• Four million women are severely assaulted per year.
(Langan Pa, Innes CA. *Preventing Domestic Violence against Women.* Washington, DC: U.S. Department of Justice, Bureau of Justice Statistics: 1986)

• Over one-third of assaults to women involve severe aggression such as punching, kicking, choking, beating up, or using a knife or a gun.
(Langan Pa, Innes CA. *Preventing Domestic Violence against Women.* Washington, DC: U.S. Department of Justice, Bureau of Justice Statistics: 1986)

- From one-fifth to one-third of all women will be physically assaulted by a partner in their lifetime.
(Frieze I H, Browne A. Violence in marriage. In: Ohlin L, Tonry M, eds. *Family Violence: Crime and Justice,* a Review of Research. Chicago, Ill: University of Chicago Press; 1989: 163-218)

- The rate of injury to women from battering surpasses that of car accidents and muggings combined.
(McClear SV, Anwar RA. The role of the emergency physician in the prevention of domestic violence. *Ann Emerg Med.* 1987: 16: 1155-1161)

- Approximately 95 percent of the victims of battering are women.
(Bureau of Justice Statistics, Report to the Nation on Crime and Justice: The Data, Washington, DC: Office of Justice Programs, U.S. Department of Justice, October 1983)

- Twenty-one percent of all women who use the hospital emergency surgical service are battered.
(Stark, E. *Wife abuse in the medical setting: an introduction for health personnel.* (Monograph ser. No 7) Rockville, MD, National Clearinghouse on Domestic Violence, April 1981)

SHE 2

What Is Abuse?

"Abuse" will be used in this definition to indicate violence inflicted upon a woman by a man with whom she is married or cohabiting. Abuse can be found among married and unmarried heterosexuals, lesbians and gays. It cuts across geographic, religious, economic, and racial barriers. Abuse is a pattern of control that a man exercises to physically harm, induce fear, prevent a woman from doing what she wishes, or force her to perform in ways she does not want to. Abuse includes physical, emotional or sexual attacks.

Physical abuse is: pushing, scratching slapping, hitting, punching, choking, kicking, holding, biting, or throwing, locking you out of the house, driving recklessly when you are in the car, throwing objects at you, threatening to hurt you with a weapon, abandoning you in dangerous places, refusing to help when you are pregnant, injured, or sick.

Emotional abuse is: ignoring your feelings, ridiculing your beliefs, withholding approval, threatening to take your children, telling you about his affairs, manipulating you with lies, threatening to leave you, taking the car keys or money, keeping you from working or going to school, humiliating you in public or private, abusing your pets or children, calling you names or driving your family or friends away.

81

Sexual abuse is: insisting that you dress in an uncomfortable sexual way, calling you sexual names like "whore," "bitch," forcing you to strip, forcing unwanted sexual acts, withholding sex, criticizing you sexually, insisting on unwanted touching, assuming you would have sex with any available man.

National Numbers

National Coalition Against Domestic Violence
(202) 638-6388

National Coalition Against Sexual Assault
(202) 483-7165

Attorney Referral Network
(800) 624-8846

SHE 4

Characteristics of Many Abused Women

For clarity, "husband" will be analogous to "cohabitator" or "partner;" "relationship" to "marriage."

1. Abused women are found in all socioeconomic levels, all educational, and all racial groups.

2. The abused woman has a martyr-like behavior; she is often a long sufferer and overloaded with the demands of others. The abused woman has difficulty nurturing herself and feels unappreciated.

3. She is often employed but is not allowed control of any finances.

4. The abused woman doesn't know how to deal with stress; she can have anxiety attacks. Usually this type of woman will feel tired and overworked. She doesn't provide enough space in her life for breaks; poor management of time and resources are quite apparent; it's hard for her to make life changes. Problem solving is very stressful.

5. She accepts "responsibility" for the batterer's violent behavior.

6. The battered woman is isolated and loses contact with her family or friends; she often feels embarrassed about her situation. This type of woman is further isolated because her partner doesn't want her to give time to friends, neighbors, relatives, or outside activities. He wants all the attention himself.

7. She suffers from guilt; this woman may feel that she deserves to be beaten because she is not able to live up to her husband's expectations.

8. The abused woman is a traditionalist about her role in the home; she strongly believes in family unity and has traditional expectations of her husband or cohabitator as the provider. This type of woman doesn't like her role and can "nag." She wants to keep the image of a socially or religiously acceptable marriage.

9. The abused woman has a low self-esteem and doesn't feel that she has much value. She is extremely critical of herself and usually of others. She doesn't have a high level of self-preservation.

10. She accepts violence in hopes that someday she will be able to change her mate. She believes that she caused the anger and violence. She usually loves her husband and wants to trust his promises that he'll reform, although this rarely happens.

11. She was emotionally neglected as a child; she was physically and/or sexually abused as a child or saw violence in her family. She could have been abused by a sibling, parent, or a relative.

12. It's difficult for the battered woman to verbalize her needs and desires to others. She has poor communication skills and has difficulty in being able to express her anger. Because she is unassertive, she can be quite manipulative. She is skilled in the art of complaining. Her complaints are usually not listened to or resolved by her partner.

13. This woman is often in denial; she often will not admit to herself that she has been physically, emotionally, or sexually abused. The abused woman may think of each incident as an "accident." She often gives herself excuses for her husband's violence. The abused woman is a great rationalizer: "He's not so bad. He's a great provider."

14. From her childhood she was taught to defer power to a male. Much of the time she feels helpless and will look for someone to help her put her life together. She does not want to take responsibility for making decisions and would rather have someone else make them. Many abused women feel comfortable in taking a "compliant" position; she has been brought up

to believe that women are weak, inferior and should submit to men in return for financial support.

15. This type of woman has sexual problems because of unresolved anger toward her abusive husband. She receives a great deal of further abuse for not performing like she used to.

16. The abused woman is often depressed. She can try to make herself less depressed with alcohol, drugs, shopping sprees, overcleaning, overeating, etc. She can contemplate suicide.

17. She is at high risk of being hit on the face or head area; during pregnancy she may be hit in the abdomen.

18. The abused woman is unable to convince her partner that accusations about her cheating on him are untrue.

19. Because she is being hit by her partner, she can hit her own child(ren) and then feel extremely sorry.

20. The abused woman is usually willing to "mother" an emotionally immature man; she is willing to sacrifice and not expose his inexcusable abuse towards her, her children, friends, relatives property, pets. This woman feels that she is expected to act more like a mother than a wife.

SHE 5

Effects of Domestic Violence on Children

Children are present in 41–55 percent of homes where police intervene in domestic violence calls.

Lenore Walker's 1984 study found that mothers who were battered were eight times more likely to hurt their children.

In a major study of more than 900 children at shelters, it was determined that 70 percent of the children were victims of physical abuse or neglect. Almost 50 percent of these children had been physically or sexually abused. This study also found that the male batterer most often abused the children.

Children in homes where abuse occurs may "indirectly" receive injuries. They may be hurt when items are thrown or weapons are used. Babies may be hurt if they are being held by their mother when the batterer strikes out.

Boys who witnessed domestic violence as children are more likely to batter their female partners as adults than boys raised in nonviolent homes.

SHE 6

Positive Phraseology For Our Children

How we incorporate our words in sentences is one of the main ingredients in fulfilling or unfulfilling relationships with our children. The following are phrases which foster positive parenting. You might consider incorporating them into your communication patterns.

- "I feel deeply about this issue."

- "Your point of view is something I want to hear."

- "I want to solve this together."

- "Let's both have a little time to think about this problem."

- "I respect your reasons."

- "Educate me about what you know about this."

- "May I share how I feel with you?"

- "Tell me what you would do if you were in my shoes?"

- "What are some of your options?"

- "I need to study your information."

- "Your behavior is having an impact on me. I feel (uneasy, angry, anxious)."

- "Can you help me understand why this is important to you?"

- "I'm listening to your words."

- "Our relationship is something I care about."

- "I want to respect your feelings."

- "How do you feel right now?"

Programmed Messages From Our Childhood

- Shame on you for thinking that!

- Why don't you act like a nice girl?

- I'm always sacrificing for you, and you are so ungrateful!

- You're driving me crazy with what you want!

- No talking back to me.

- I don't care how you feel.

- Don't get angry with me. I'll give you something to get angry about.

- Don't cry so much. It bothers me.

- Why don't you do it this way?

- Can't you get anything done on time?

- Hurry and grow older. I can't wait until you move out.

- You're not good enough to do that. Quit thinking so big.

- I wish that you had never been born.

- I don't want to hear you.

- Don't get so emotional.

- Don't ask so many stupid questions.

- Don't tell other people about this family's business.

- Just look at my directions.

- You're so self-centered.

- Don't discuss the family with outsiders.

- You caused all your problems.

- We won't love you if you do that.

- You'll never get anywhere.

- It didn't really hurt you that badly.

- I don't believe you.

I Have the Right

1. I have the right to be in a safe, nonviolent home. I do not have to accept physical, emotional, or sexual abuse.

2. I have the right to make mistakes. I do not have to be told that I am inadequate.

3. I have the right to make my own decisions and be respected for my intelligence. I have the right to pursue my own interests.

4. I have the right to focus on my needs. I do not have to participate in a relationship that does not encourage my well-being.

5. I have the right to challenge another and to discuss the problems this person's behavior creates for me.

6. I have the right to believe that I have a good memory and can remember events accurately.

7. I have the right to change my own mind.

8. I have the right not to answer a question.

9. I have the right to care for myself. I do not have to feel guilty or responsible. I am not obligated to fulfill the needs of a man who was mistreated emotionally or physically by his parents, served time in jail or has a drug or drinking problem.

10. I have the right to have a man arrive on time. I do not have to accept excuses for behavior that is inexcusable.

11. I have the right to express how I feel. My feelings are important and deserve to be listened to.

12. I have the right to have trust agreements kept with me regarding my body, my emotions, and my child or children.

13. I have the right to have a man who is sexually faithful.

14. I have the right to participate in the process of making rules that will affect my life.

15. I have the right to be proud of myself and my achievements.

16. I have the right to provide a healthy environment for myself and my child or children.

Characteristics of Many Male Batterers

For clarity, "wife" will be analogous to "cohabitator" or "partner;" "relationship" to "marriage."

1. He is found in all socioeconomic levels, all age groups, and all racial groups. Many batterers have police records.

2. He has a low self-esteem. Many are insecure about their worth as providers, husbands or sexual partners.

3. He blames others for his actions; he has poor impulse control and can have explosive temper outbursts. He has a low tolerance for frustration.

4. He doesn't believe his violent behavior should have negative interpretations; he has no awareness of, or guilt for violating his wife's boundaries.

5. He has a family history of domestic violence; he witnessed a "significant other" being physically or emotionally abused. The batterer has not acquired the necessary social lesson that beating up a woman is wrong.

6. He can employ some of the following weapons, besides fists and feet: guns, knives, a broom, a belt, a brush, a pillow (to smother), a hot iron, lighted cigarettes.

7. His expectations of the relationship are unrealistic; he expects his wife to conform to his fantasies; his expectations are often unspoken. He has insatiable childlike needs and believes that his partner or children "ought to" be this and this, do that and that. The batterer is often not satisfied with the efforts of those he lives with; he often relates that he has been let down.

8. He is emotionally dependent on his wife and children; when his partner threatens separation, he can exert control over his mate by threatening homicide and/or suicide.

9. The abuser has a high level of job dissatisfaction, underemployment, or unemployment that leads to feelings of inadequacy and inability to provide for his family according to societal stereotypes.

10. He has poor communication skills and accepts violence as a viable method of problem solving; the abuser sees it as an acceptable means of maintaining a family. He makes sure that his partner will not escape by keeping car keys, money, ripping the phone out of the wall, etc.

11. He can have an unpredictable and confusing personality.

12. He is a traditionalist who believes in male supremacy in the family; the batterer thinks that he is in charge, and that women should be submissive and content to be controlled. The abu-

sive male believes that his forcible behavior isn't a crime; it is aimed at keeping the family intact. He frequently keeps his partner isolated from society—as well as from friends, neighbors, and even family.

13. He tends to be jealous and can make accusations against his mate that he has been "cheated on." He can voice great fear that his partner will abandon him. The batterer can employ clever espionage tactics against his mate: checking the gas mileage when his partner does errands, eavesdropping on his partner's telephone conversations, etc.

14. He can plead that his violent behavior has great potential for reform; he can make many promises and then forget that he made them.

15. He can inflict invisible injuries mostly to the head. Many abusers can cause injury to the abdominal area during pregnancy.

16. Those closest to him know that he is characterized by depression and self pity. The batterer often feels that no one cared about him in his childhood. He believes that his marriage is not providing the caring he needs right now.

17. His use of alcohol or drugs is sometimes associated with the abuse of his partner; their usage is often used as an excuse rather than a cause.

SHE 10

I Let an Abuser Know That I Am a Victim:

1. I send out signals to an abuser that I am a victim primarily through my communication patterns. I alert him that I fear power through my tendency to cry. I send out weakness signals by pointing out my shortcomings to him. I volunteer damaging information about myself. Because I feel helpless, I feel it is all right to rely on him. My demands, however, are more than he can, or will, fulfill.

2. From my childhood, I coped by adopting a martyr stance for relating to others. It is often difficult for me to utilize assertive strategies in my adult interpersonal relationships with men. My communication has repeated patterns of trying to appease or second-guess him. Mind reading is an art for me. I am often supersensitive to his needs. My specialty is trying to accommodate what he wants. I let him know that he is more powerful than I am.

3. Apologizing or saying, "I'm sorry," relates an impotent position to him: "I'm weak." "I'm not worth much." "Please don't hurt me." This communicates to him that I am not powerful and includes a plea for leniency. It is difficult for me

to defend my rights or insist on limits. My boundaries and limits of tolerance are poorly communicated to him.

4. Repressing my own needs and feelings is an adaptive behavior pattern that I carry over from my childhood. Saying "no" is almost an impossibility because I desire approval and find it difficult to offend him. It is hard to acknowledge my personal needs because I learned to regard them as an imposition. I have a difficult time making decisions. I fear making the wrong decisions and paying the consequences. I do not feel that I have a rightful heritage to a satisfying life. My behavior is one of learned helplessness and a position that suffering is a way of life.

5. When I sense that I am the center of critical attention from my partner, I am easily wounded. I fear criticism because my self-esteem depends solely on his estimation of me. I am very self-involved, constantly checking my progress or success by seeing myself in his eyes. I am thrown off-center by what he thinks of me. I give him the power to affect my view of myself. If he is happy with me, I am happy with myself; if he is not, I am not. I am an approval addict who spends so much time evaluating my behavior that when I am criticized by him, it is almost too much to bear.

6. I am terrified by his hostility and do not believe that I should ever get angry. I have a great tolerance for emotional pain. I can put up with a lot of inexcusable behavior from the man in my life. I can be suffocatingly sweet. To feel safe with my partner, I am compliant and become what I believe he wants me to be. My self-esteem rests on being affirmed by him. I have an imaginary, idealized self, a perfect self. I find myself angry and resentful for not being perfect. I have a difficult time accepting myself as ordinary, or mediocre. I am critical of myself and others. Treating myself with care and a sense of self-preservation is not something that comes naturally to me within a relationship. I find myself attempting to drive painful anxiety about my relationship underground with self-destructive addictions: alcoholism, drugs, shopping sprees, overeating, or compulsive cleaning.

7. I guard vigilantly against expressing my anger and pay particular attention to the expression on his face and the tone of his voice. I either turn my anger inward and get depressed. Or I express it inappropriately in a hostile and explosive manner. I can't tolerate uncertainty. It makes me feel very uncomfortable; I have a strong urge to make everything all right. Sometimes when I try to correct things I make them worse.

Suggested Reading on Domestic Violence

Martin, Del, *Battered Wives,* Volcano Press, Inc., Volcano, CA, 1981.

NiCarthy, Ginny, *Getting Free: You Can End Abuse and Take Back Your Life,* Seal Press, Seattle, WA, 1986.

NiCarthy, Ginny, *The Ones Who Got Away: Women Who Left Abusive Partners,* Seal Press, Seattle, WA, 1987.

NiCarthy, Ginny; et al, *Talking It Out: A Guide to Groups for Abused Women,* Seal Press, Seattle, WA, 1984.

NiCarthy, Ginny, *You Can Be Free: An Easy to Read Handbook for Abused Women,* Seal Press, Seattle, WA, 1989.

Shainess, Natalie, *Sweet Suffering: Woman as Victim,* MacMillan, 1984.

Sonkin, Ph.D., Daniel & Durphy, M.D., Michael, *Learning to Live Without Violence: A Handbook for Men,* Volcano Press, Inc., Volcano, CA, 1989.

Sonkin, Ph.D., Daniel & Durphy, M.D., Michael, *Learning to Live Without Violence: A Worktape for Men,* (two C-60 cassettes) Volcano Press, Inc., Volcano, CA, 1989.

Kilgore, Nancy, *Sourcebook for Working With Battered Women,* Volcano Press, Inc., Volcano, CA, 1993.

The Volcano Press titles listed above may be ordered from your local bookstore, or directly from the publisher:

Volcano Press, Inc.
P.O. Box 270-E
Volcano, CA 95689-0270

Phone: 209-296-3445
FAX: 209-296-4515

Please write or phone for our complete domestic violence catalog.

QUESTIONNAIRE
Have You Been Abused?

The following questionnaire can help you identify whether you are an abused woman. Your courage and willingness to fill out the questionnaire indicates your willingness to want a positive life. Consider your present or past relationship. Even though you may not currently be in a relationship, you might still be recovering from abuse.

Circle Yes or No

1. **Yes No** Do you find yourself trying to drive painful fear and anxiety underground with self-destructive addictions: alcoholism, shopping sprees, overeating, negative relationships, compulsive cleaning, drugs?

2. **Yes No** Has he locked you out of the house, taken the car keys or money, humiliated you in public, abused your pets or children, or driven your family or friends away?

3. **Yes No**   Do you feel that you live in fear because he has pushed, scratched, slapped, hit, punched, choked, kicked, tightly held, bit, or thrown you in your relationship?

4. **Yes No**   Are you terrified of his anger? Do you keep a vigilant guard to be perfect so he won't get angry?

5. **Yes No**   Do you have a communication style with him of trying to appease or second-guess him?

6. **Yes No**   Has he driven recklessly when you are in the car, thrown objects at you, threatened to hurt you with a weapon, abandoned you in dangerous places, refused to help when you are pregnant, injured, or sick?

7. **Yes No**   Do you seem to have this martyr stance of: *"Even if you step on me, I will still love you. I am giving, loving, and forgiving?"*

8. **Yes No**   Do you find it difficult to face reality in your relationship and often find yourself fantasizing about what it could be like?

9. **Yes No**   Do you lie awake worrying about your abusive relationship?

10. **Yes No** Are you embarrassed to discuss your relationship situation with your friends or relatives?

11. **Yes No** Do you withdraw from friends, relatives and outside activities when your relationship is not working?

Count the number of "yes" responses that you gave and compare that number to the breakdown below. If you feel that you are currently involved in an abusive relationship, do not lose hope. There are many resources in your neighborhood that you can turn to for help.

1–2 You are probably affected by "love dependency" (a preoccupation with a relationship).

3–6 You are suffering from abuse and should start examining what is happening in the relationship.

7–9 You should seriously start examining your relationship more closely as you are showing signs of being involved in abuse. Abuse is definitely the issue.

10–11 Crisis intervention needed! Seek individual help from a counselor familiar with abuse. Joint therapy is not appropriate!

SHE 13

Shirley

Shirley grew up in the south and is still very much a traditional Southern woman in some ways. At forty-five, she has been a suburban housewife and mother of two for twenty-five years.

Shirley speaks of emotional abuse and sexual humiliation as the intolerable aspects of life with Clarence, her engineer husband. Only when questioned specifically about it does she say offhandedly that yes, he was physically abusive too. One of the things he did to her was to push her down the stairs when she was pregnant.

He criticized her cooking, her housekeeping and everything about her. He was so rude to everyone that they had no friends. Over the years, Shirley became convinced that she was incompetent to do anything, so that now, six months after leaving him, she worries about whether she'll even be able to rake the leaves adequately.

Shirley had several strokes, which she attributed to the stress of living with Clarence's abuse, yet even long hospitalizations didn't worry her enough to propel her out of the marriage. But when Clarence put their thirteen-year old daughter out of the house, Shirley finally gained the strength to separate from him. After six months she is slowly learning to re-gain her ability to handle everyday tasks, her health has vastly improved and she's considering taking up the nursing school classes that she dropped twenty-five years ago.

Depression

Symptoms of Depression:

- Feelings of despair, sadness, hopelessness
- Difficulty sleeping, early wakening, difficulty getting out of bed
- Thoughts of "ending it all," "why bother?"
- Restlessness, irritability, guilt
- Low self-esteem or self criticism
- Eating disturbance; usually loss of appetite or weight gain
- Fatigue, decreased energy, low motivation
- Memory loss; concentration diminished
- Loss of interest and pleasure in activities once enjoyed

Common Causes of Depression

We are apt to feel depressed when we:

- Are physically fatigued, ill, or run down
- Have lost a dream or a goal
- Feel guilty about something we have done, or haven't done
- Have been hurt by someone, have lost someone we love, have gone from a situation where we were happy to one that seems to hold no hope
- Feel lonely or inferior

Afterword

Dear Reader:

Hopefully, after finishing this book, your life will change. It is my hope that after reading my personal journey through domestic violence, you can search for the elements of personal transformation to discover hope and the ability to love with a true sense of safety.

There is an old Chinese saying that each generation builds a road for the next. As women, the road has not been well built for us, and I believe it incumbent upon us, in our generation, to build a road for the next generation of women. A new world is dawning for us to make positive changes for ourselves and for our children.

We must get ready for the storm that will rip through the doors of so many homes. Domestic violence is rapidly increasing. You are a light that can help another woman believe she can walk alone, or toward a positive love relationship. Know that you are valuable.

Nancy Kilgore

My Personal Notes

My Personal Notes

My Personal Notes

My Personal Notes

My Personal Notes

My Personal Notes